CRUISING
WEATHER

By the same author

Wind and Sailing Boats
Weather Forecasting Ashore and Afloat
Instant Weather Forecasting
Instant Wind Forecasting
Wind Pilot
Basic Windcraft

CRUISING WEATHER

Alan Watts

Illustrated by Peter Milne

Copyright © Alan Watts 1982

First published in Great Britain 1982 by
NAUTICAL BOOKS
An imprint of Macmillan London Ltd
4 Little Essex Street
London WC2R 3LF

Associated companies in Auckland, Dallas,
Delhi, Dublin, Hong Kong, Johannesburg,
Lagos, Manzini, Melbourne, Nairobi,
New York, Singapore, Tokyo, Washington
and Zaria

Composition in Imprint by
Filmtype Services Limited,
Scarborough, North Yorkshire

Printed in Hong Kong

British Library Cataloguing in Publication Data

Watts, Alan
    Cruising weather.
    1. Weather forecasting   2. Yachts and yachting
    I. Title
    551.6'3'0247971   QC995

    ISBN 0-333-32217-7

Contents

Introduction

If you sail a cruising boat you sail the waters and experience the winds and weather that are the subject of this book. You buy a boat to have fun and get away from it all and so, just because of that, why should you also have to become a meteorologist? The answer is that you do not, but the coastal strip of water that is the traditional haunt of the cruiser is potentially one of the most dangerous from a weather point of view.

The deep-sea crews, when they see the barometer plummeting and the white horses gathering, secure and head for the open sea. They are tough and disciplined and know what to expect before they 'sign on'. The creek and estuary sailor, on the other hand, has the friendly land to protect him from the wind and the waves, and if conditions get too tough he can pull up somewhere and sit it out.

The cruising sailor can often do neither of these things. The sand and shingle bars of harbours are the most notorious places to be when the wind is rising. If you leave it too late you may not be able to get back in, or if you do run the gauntlet it can be a very hairy ride. Furthermore, one or more of your crew members may not be all that experienced or you may have taken someone along for the ride who, with others, may suffer badly from seasickness and so become a positive handicap.

It is a fact that the coastal shallows make the biggest and most chaotic wave patterns and if the wind is on-shore there is always the fear of being driven on to a lee shore. If the wind blows roughly along the line of the coast it may well be stronger there than elsewhere and if at the same time the tide runs against it, the seaway can become almost impossible to meet. If this sounds like a catalogue of disasters designed to put the fear of God into you, then all I can say is that all these things and more happen in the coastal waters where most of the cruising, fishing, day-sailing and off-the-beach dinghy sailors meet and they give a good enough reason for getting to know something about the weather and how it develops.

However I do believe that most sailing people only want to know enough met to get by and keep out of trouble – and no one will blame them for that. Therefore this book starts with forecasts – just listening to them will warn you to act prudently. You may miss a tide that someone else hauled out on, but as the wind whistles through the rigging, halyards flap against masts and waves slap against the immobile hull you will be glad you took the trouble to listen to the forecast.

On the other hand, when you are more experienced and have more knowledge of your limits, you can set out when the forecast goes for 'winds, fresh to strong' and make a perfectly secure passage. Or you may gain enough local knowledge to say that the forecast has got the timing wrong for your area and so slip from one port to another between blows. That entails a more developed weather sense and it means adding to the forecasts with knowledge and observations of your own. The second part of this book helps to supplement the forecasts with tried and tested methods that will stand you in good stead wherever you may sail.

Finally you may want to understand the weather more deeply so that you know why, as well as knowing what and how. This information is left until Part Two because you will have already gained a good deal of empirical knowledge before you ever feel the need to probe more deeply into meteorology. However you will need this knowledge for the various proficiency tests that can be taken these days and these tests are, when you have successfully passed them, a great fillip to your morale. Even if you do not pass them they are a spur to gaining essential knowledge.

Eventually, however, whether you intend to pit yourself against the worst of the elements and the toughest tests or whether you just intend to cruise gently from A to B for the fun and relaxation of it, you should be able to find some help with your weather doubts and worries in this book. At least I hope so – here's to some happy and carefree cruising!

Part One

1 About forecasting today

Some years ago when the author was himself a weather forecaster, the computer was a revolution yet to come and every met station had to have a full complement of meteorological assistants to read the observations and transfer their coded figures into plotted symbols around the station circles on the weather charts before they could be drawn up. Since then there has been a remarkable revolution in the collection, storage and regurgitation of weather observations from all over the world, and in the way that the finished weather charts -- which once had to be drawn and analyzed by hand -- are sent to interested recipients who have the necessary receiving apparatus.

The forecasting services have been revolutionized by the high-speed computer and the facsimile machine. In the Central Forecast Office (CFO) at Bracknell in Berkshire, Britain has one of the biggest, fastest computers in the world and uses it to store vast quantities of observations and charts as well as to work with complex mathematical relationships and throw up forecasts of what the isobars will look like as much as 72 hours ahead. Bracknell is more than a forecasting centre; it is a telecommunications centre and one of a worldwide network of so-called 'regional hubs' which collect weather data from their surrounding observation centres which form the spokes of the wheel.

Bracknell is just one of three such hubs in Western Europe, the other two being Paris and Offenbach. These hubs are links in a communication chain that stretches across the world between two major centres in the northern hemisphere -- Washington for the western half and Moscow for the eastern. Melbourne is the centre for the whole of the southern hemisphere.

Each centre and hub has a computer which accepts, stores and processes information. Some of its stored information is sent on to the other hubs and centres on a routine basis, and each can be interrogated to obtain observations or other information required by any other. Much of the traffic is by radio via geostationary communication satellites hovering over suitable fixed points on the Equator. Thus each regional hub has all the

figure 1.1

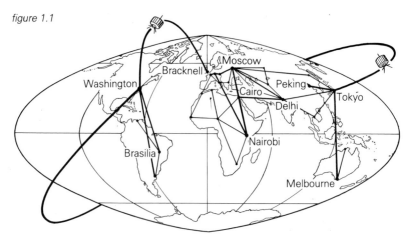

The world meteorological communication network with the major oceans spanned by geostationary relay satellites.

information passing along the communication link stored on its high speed computer, and by organizing a strict schedule of all kinds of weather messages the telecommunication centres can be automated (see figure 1.1).

A regional hub such as Bracknell collects information from the many met stations throughout Britain. Each station is manned by meteorological assistants, who act as observers, and by forecasters, although only about two-thirds of Britain's stations report on a regular 24-hour basis. The observations are taken just before the hour and sent in an international five-figure reporting code to a regional collecting centre – a subsidiary hub in fact. The subsidiary hub collates its clutch of reports and sends them on to the regional hub which in turn feeds them automatically to its communication computer for onward routing to interested recipients. At the same time the forecasters on the out stations scan down the apparently meaningless groups of figures that are chattering off their teleprinters. These figures are the coded observations, the more local of which were collected a bare ten minutes ago, which have been sent back in collated fashion under their regional headings from the regional hub. The observations for many British stations are in the hands of the local forecasters between ten and twenty minutes past the hour. Thus if you want to ring a met office for the latest information it is best to make your call between half past and ten to the hour. You will then have given the forecaster time to digest the import of the latest observations but will not interfere with the collection of the observations at the next hour.

In the interim, chart-plotting machines in the CFO automatically transfer the observations on the computer to the smallest mesh of the weather chart complex – the hourly charts. These charts can be used to follow the progress of weather systems from hour to hour, and they are broadcast to out stations via the fax machine, the most important adjunct to local forecasting yet to be introduced.

Once upon a time local forecasters had to rely on their assistants to take the observations and transfer them laboriously by hand to the blank charts. Some of this work may still be necessary, but today charts roll off the fax machine hour after hour, some with the available observations plotted and ready to be drawn up with isobars and fronts. The out station forecaster has not had all his skill pre-empted by his superiors at the regional hub, but the drudgery of manually plotting the observations at many local met offices has been eliminated enabling a forecaster to perform a perfectly adequate forecasting service with just his knowledge and a fax machine to provide the raw material. Another important advance is that a met assistant, precluded from giving his own forecasts, may read you the latest forecast from the fax.

In a highly important experiment at the trials before the 1968 Acapulco Olympics, David Houghton (now a deputy director of the Meteorological Office) and the author were able to give a weather forecast service to the competing crews solely by virtue of having the necessary information churning off a facsimile machine installed especially for the occasion at the Royal Motor Yacht Club at Poole. Subsequently David accompanied the British Olympic Team to Acapulco performing a valuable service to the competing crews who were sailing in strange tropical surroundings and set a pattern that many other countries have followed. Today any yacht or club can have a lightweight fax machine installed and so tap a vast reservoir of charts both actual and forecast, outlooks for days ahead, satellite cloud analyses etc coming over the airwaves (see page 42).

The charts on which the main forecasting is based are those that are drawn using the midnight and midday observations. These are also the times when the upper air is sounded by radiosonde ascents. No matter what time it may be throughout the world all countries draw their major charts, and make their main upper air soundings at the same global times of 0001 and 1200 GMT (the main synoptic hours). Washington, for example, will start drawing its '1200 GMT' chart with observations taken at 0700 EST in its own area and later fill in with observations that have been made simultaneously by all other met stations throughout the entire world, whatever their zone time differences may be. The other two main synoptic hours are 0600 and 1800 GMT when only radar wind observations are made in the upper atmosphere. Charts of actual weather are called analyses (see figure 1.2b).

To forecast a day ahead by the old methods involved just two levels of the atmosphere – the surface and the pressure level of 500 millibars. Complex rules were devised to relate features of these two levels so as to reveal when depressions would deepen or form, and other important

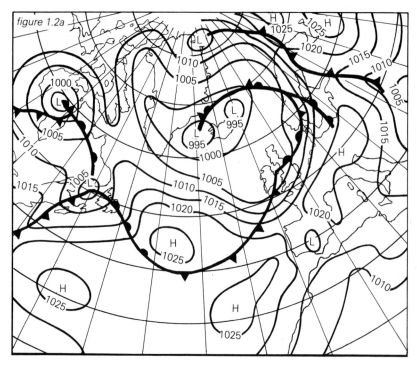

Surface forecasting. The 30 hours ahead forecast chart for 0600 GMT Tuesday 14 August 1979 based on the midnight Sunday analysis.

future events of the coming hours. Some of these rules have been simplified for your use in Section 40.

The computer has now taken over this work and immensely extended it so that instead of marrying two levels – which is all the human forecasters could hope to do in the time available – the forecast model on which the computer works has no less than ten levels. This allows for the interaction of air motions from the surface up to 17 km (9 Nmi) which is about the highest level to which all the sonde balloons can be expected to get before exploding (most go to over 12 Nmi). Luckily the atmospheric motions in the upper air decks are less complex than those at the surface as they are largely unaffected by surface features. So the equations that govern atmospheric motion in most of the ten layers work better than they would in the surface layer and help to predict the surface pressure pattern.

The human forecaster with his great powers of decision can intervene as the computer does its work of first averaging the actual, but irregularly spaced, observations it has on stream so as to give itself values spaced over a regular 300 km (162 Nmi) grid.

The forecaster's intervention allows analysis of satellite pictures to have a hand in refining the initial situation and also, on a more mundane level, if the computer shows it thinks a pressure centre is at point A and the forecaster is pretty certain that it is at point B, he can tell the computer to change its values in that region accordingly. Between them human and machine come to an agreement as to the initial set of data and the forecasting process starts. The computer works on forecasting the future values of temperature, pressure etc at each half hour ahead at the grid points which you might imagine as a regular matrix of grains of mustard seed in a nine-decker sandwich.

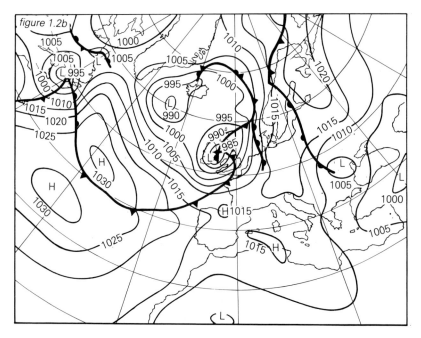

The actual chart for the same time as the forecast (above). *This was the morning after the great Fastnet storm. The intensity of the storm was not foreseen by the computer working so far ahead, but the general situation was very accurately forecast. The cold front is a little further on into England, but not much. The warm front loops across into Scandinavia as forecast. The 1005 mb isobar (on fax charts the interval between isobars is 5 mb) cuts through Britain rather than going through the southeast corner, which is not far out. If someone with a hunch had put some rings of isobars round the point where warm and cold fronts meet over the northern part of the Irish Sea they would have got the Fastnet low's position almost exact for that time. Note also how, across the other side of the Atlantic, the low over the Gulf of St Lawrence and the mid-Atlantic highs are in the right place.*

Because of the overloading of communication channels it is over three hours after the synoptic hour (0001 or 1200 GMT) before all the observations are in and the forecasting process can start. Once under way it takes even a very fast computer over an hour and a half to do the complex calculations. So all the information to draw the forecast charts (prognoses) for 24 hours ahead is not on the computer until five hours after the synoptic hour. However once the machine is at work it does not rest at a day's predictions – it can go on to a limit of six days ahead.

So, while there is initial delay in arriving at a short-term forecast, modern techniques enable a new degree of confidence to be given to three-day and six-day forecasts. Of course not all the tricks of the atmosphere are fully known to meteorologists who must constantly refine their techniques and the computer programme. And the computer does not do away with the acumen and knowledge of the human forecasters who man airfields and weather centres and whose interest is more local and often covers a much shorter range. It is to these that the mariner will often be speaking as he attempts to discover if his passage is wise or not.

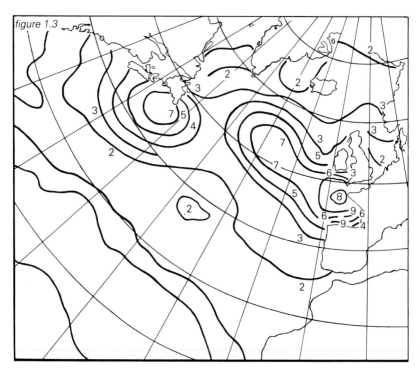

Wave forecasting. The 12 hours ahead wave height and direction computer forecast for 1800 GMT the same day as figs 1.2. The heights are in metres. State of sea in Biscay was considered to be in the 'high' bracket.

figure 1.4

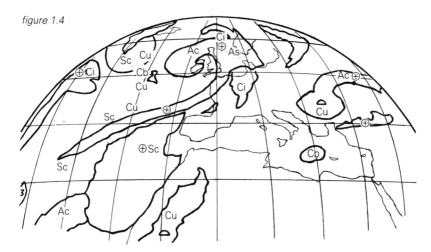

Diagram of cloud over the northern hemisphere as seen by the geostationary satellite Meteosat above the Equator and on the Greenwich meridian. This is an analyzed reproduction of the important features taken from the picture broadcast to receiving stations at 0600 GMT 14 August 1979.

The computer also works on a shorter range, forecasting from a finer grid of points over a smaller time module of 12½-minute steps. Surface pressure charts are produced for each six hours up to 36 hours ahead. Not all these prognoses will be sent out as charts. Many will be stored on the computer to be run off as required. For example, the facsimile schedule broadcast by Bracknell for the use of ships at sea includes actual surface charts for 24 hours ahead of those times. Also available are surface charts (surface prognoses) for 30, 48 and 72 hours ahead of the major synoptic hours (see figure 1.2a).

The computer has another task – that of forecasting the wave situation (wave prognosis) and actual wave analyses plus forecasts of state of sea for 24 and 48 hours ahead are broadcast via facsimile (see figure 1.3). In addition, twice a day a chart, a nephanalysis (see figure 1.4), showing the cloud conditions revealed by the satellite cloud pictures is broadcast.

Such information is now becoming available to the small craft mariner via light, compact facsimile recievers, but as the outlay may be around a thousand pounds only a few yachts will as yet be fitted with it and then perhaps only for special races or passages. However, facsimile is the most likely way in which the impasse that exists between central hub forecasting centres and the public may be broken. The problem is that forecasting centres have computers bursting with useful information that they cannot send to the interested recipients. Try plotting a chart from the shipping forecast and comparing your efforts with the original and forecast charts on which it was based. It is then you realize that a radio description is a very inadequate substitute for a drawn-up chart.

Listeners to shipping forecasts should bear in mind the schedule on which they are produced. The shipping forecast read at 0015 on BBC Radio 4 (200 kHz), for example, is based on observations taken over six hours earlier, ie on the 1800 analysis chart of the North Atlantic area. The outlook period is guided by the shape of the prognosis chart for 24 hours ahead ie 1800 of the day the forecast is read. So while the broad features are usually correctly forecast smaller local effects may change the weather either in time or severity. A movement in a pressure system towards intensification that started after the issue of the previous forecast (which would have been post 1705 – see schedule below) would have had over seven hours to cook and that can be a disastrously long time.

It is not enough, when there is a possibility of trouble, for the small craft crew to listen to a shipping forecast and then forget it until the next one. A case in point was the Fastnet gale of 1979 (whose meteorology will be used as an example in several places in this book). The low approaching Ireland (see photograph on page 17) only showed real signs of its final severity after the broadcast of the 1750 shipping forecast. Thus only those with their ears to the gale warnings from Radio 4 or a coast radio station were aware of the imminent severity of the storm.

The schedule for issue of shipping forecasts from the BBC is as follows:

Forecast issued by the Central Forecasting Office	Time of BBC broadcast	Based on analysis and prognosis for
2330	0015	1800
0530	0625	0001
1255	1355	0600
1705	1750	1200

Right: Modern techniques of electronic enhancement (sectoring) bring out the features of satellite cloud pictures in great detail. This is the visible (rather than infra-red) image from TIROS N on the afternoon of 11 September 1980 when on its 9863rd orbit. Compare the detail here with that of fig 3.2 which is unsectored. The great swirl over the British Isles is an occluding depression with its cold front trailing back into the Atlantic. The warm front cloud covers the eastern side of Britain and veils of cirrostratus cloud are visible over the leading edges of the warm front. Craft sailing in the eastern North Sea would have seen haloes about the sun. Behind the cold front the woolly lumps are cumulonimbus (shower) clouds while over the Dutch and German coastline cloud streets of cumulus have formed. At centre bottom similar features inland from the Baie de la Seine can be seen. (Photo by courtesy of the University of Dundee Electronics Laboratory.)

2 The upper air

When you are new to weather study the most important single advance in your understanding comes when you automatically begin to think about the weather in three dimensions. The atmosphere is not deep – the layer in which weather occurs is just ten miles thick – but all the early warning signs are above our heads. It is rare for surface weather to give much warning of change, but the clouds spewed out by fronts and troughs, or the blue skies kindled by sinking air are effects of the high atmosphere. Later in Section 40 some rules are propounded which will help readers grasp the import of the changes that occur at altitude, for the forecasts of coming change for good or bad are written in the sky.

The cruising yachtsman will see the pool of sky around him and for practical purposes that pool has a radius of some 200 miles depending on the visibility and the cloud that gets in the way. However cloud that appears on the horizon, even in conditions of very good visibility, is difficult to interpret and even the glasses may not help much. Thus the early warning from the upper air has to come from inferences in the recognizable clouds that are visible. Again that will be gone into in greater detail in Section 40. For now here's how the professionals do it.

Twice a day a network of upper air stations throughout the world send radiosonde balloons up to sound the atmosphere to about 10 nautical miles (Nmi) high. They send back information on temperature, pressure and humidity and the observations are plotted on special charts called tephigrams, so-called from the two major co-ordinates on which they are drawn, namely temperature T and entropy ϕ. The latter quantity is related to the way rising air cools or sinking air warms up and to the experienced meteorologist the tephigram is one of the most useful tools at his disposal, enabling him to estimate the amount of cloud and its height, find fronts, forecast tomorrow's maximum temperature as well as indicating when thunderstorms are likely to occur. The general public is only likely to be able to obtain tephigrams by having a fax machine or via a telecopier service and then they demand a great deal of knowledge to interpret their messages. They are definitely tools for the professional.

A column of cold air is dense and one of warm air is lighter, so the distance above the surface at which a pressure of say 500 millibars will be found is lower in the cold air than it is in the warm air. Because of this the upper air charts are drawn for single pressure values (again, say 500 mb) and this surface undulates like rolling country. Over cold columns it dips down into shallow valleys and over warmer regions it swells up into domes. Because of the upper air chart's closeness to the undulations of gently rolling land the lines which connect positions all of one height are called contours, for example, 'contours of the 500 mb surface'. The surface chart is different because its 'contours' are lines of equal pressure and not height. However it is a fact that the contours on these upper air charts act just as isobars do on surface charts, giving the speed and direction of the wind at their level. Upper winds blow along the contours just as surface winds blow along the isobars (see figure 2.1). Thus the contour charts are of great use to forecasters as they give a general (ie synoptic) view of the winds at any level as well as telling the experienced eye where the air is warmer and where it is colder than average.

The laborious plotting of contour charts is not as important to the forecaster as it was, because today radiosonde information is fed straight to the computer to enable it to start forecasting on the basis of accurate

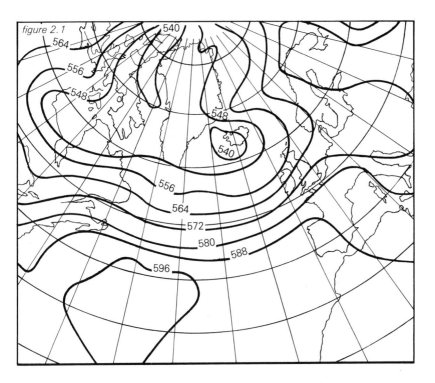

figure 2.1

Forecasting the upper winds. The 48 hours ahead forecast of the contours of the pressure level of 500 mb for 1200 GMT on Monday 13 August 1979. The closed contours over Iceland and the Atlantic show that the surface low and high respectively in these positions are not going to move. So the 'race-track' between them will continue to push lows towards Britain. The figures 596 mean 5960 metres is the height of this contour along which the pressure everywhere is 500 mb.

observations of pressure, temperature and humidity, at each of the ten standard pressure levels.

The radiosonde balloon is followed by radar and from its track the wind speed and direction at standard levels are obtained. Upper winds are observed four times a day as balloons, without instruments but carrying radar reflectors, are released and tracked between the radiosonde ascents.

While very little of this information filters through to the non-professional it is certainly the upper air data that gives birth to the future surface chart and so controls the forecast. This is perhaps the most significant of all the modern developments in forecasting techniques.

Some upper air data can be of use to the yachtsman. For example, depressions tend to move with the wind at the pressure level of 700 mb

(10,000 ft) and when a depression is moving in, knowledge of the wind at this level (by phone from a met station) in a position near the depression can help to give an idea of where it is going to track.

The upper winds will tell the forecaster where the jetstream is and a strong jet across, or to the north of, your venue is a danger position because vigorous depressions tend to develop south of the jets. The forecaster will have clues as to where the jet is likely to migrate over the next few days and so whether bad weather is more or less likely to be born in the path of your projected cruise or race.

The upper air charts also locate the anticyclones whose circulations extend to high levels and which therefore cannot travel. These are the blocking anticyclones and a block lying immobile over any area indicates days or even weeks of fine weather in summer, but on its flanks it often indicates unseasonal and nasty weather. It helps to know if there are any blocks near you because the blocks certainly control the whole area under their domination taking the depressions and guiding them round the periphery of the blocking high – often to places which otherwise would be having much better weather.

In this context the lows whose circulations extend to great heights are also ones that are not on the move either and they produce cyclonic weather in the areas under their sway. The upper air charts show the forecasters where the rings of contours aloft coincide roughly with the surface rings of isobars and indicate a quasi-stationary area of low pressure. Such cyclonic areas produce days or even weeks of unseasonal weather in summer with much cloud, a trend towards intermittent rain that may have a thundery tendency and trough-lines of showers and squalls. A favourite place for these lows in summer is south of Iceland or over the northern seas and other lows curve into them and reinforce them so that should their circulations extend as far south as Britain and France much of Europe suffers from a poor summer.

3 The real forecast

So the computer has solved all the problems of forecasting? Would that it had; it is unlikely that it will ever do so completely.

What the forecasting computer does is analyze the large-scale atmospheric motions and print them out as the bare bones of an isobaric skeleton of the real weather. This still needs to be clothed with clouds and fronts, with temperatures and many other meteorological elements by the knowledge and experience of the human forecaster. Certainly the computer can indicate the likely formation of depressions before they appear on any chart. It shows where the isobars may get tight enough in a couple of days' time to produce a gale, but it is not infallible in any of these predictions. What it does do is provide greater confidence in the long and short range periods that certain changes will take place in the weather patterns. Confidence that would once have been totally lacking when the forecasters did not have enough time to run their ideas on through a sequence of time-consuming chart-drawing operations, to see how the actual chart might change in the next two or three days. It also makes for more confidence in the short term as well, but not so much in those tricky weather situations when conditions are changing rapidly.

Indeed the computer suffers from a very important drawback – it must not be given too much leeway to introduce sudden change into its predictions. The computer cannot yet handle the sharp changes that occur across fronts, for example, and so it will draw well rounded troughs of isobars where in fact it should be drawing vee-shaped wedges of them. Here the human forecaster comes to the rescue. The fact is that if the computer were made more highly strung it might well develop a computerized form of mental instability with all the unpredictability of action that goes with such states. So it is purposely kept under a form of sedation so that what it produces is as solid and dependable as can be expected.

It must be stated quite firmly that there are periods when the predictions of the computer do not foretell the way the weather will change. Small wave depressions may be missed by it, but such waves can, and do, make for a great deal of worry in the minds of the crew at sea who see a situation they expected to be set fair deteriorating and they have no way of knowing how long the deterioration may last, or of what severity it will be. Often such waves simply produce rain or showers for longer than was expected and the wind does not get up very much, but there are other waves which deepen and produce locally strong to gale winds when nothing above Force 4 was expected. It is worth noting that a wave depression which enters the English Channel from the Atlantic is a very probable candidate to become a significant disturbance. It may not develop greatly, but the yacht who sees itself in the path of the deterioration often has no way of knowing that – and it must be faced that sometimes the forecasters are not very sure either.

Other disturbances that may slip through the net and suddenly and unexpectedly rejuvenate are to be found in September and October approaching the western shores of Britain or France. These are old hurricanes that have spent their fury on the American side and have recurved across the Atlantic. By the time they approach Europe they are demoted to lows, but an injection of cold air into them can, and does, turn them sometimes into vigorous autumn cyclones that ravage the western shores of England and Ireland, or they may slip down across the Brest peninsula into France.

Despite this the forecasters have a great deal of help that is denied the general public. They can locate thunderstorms, for example, using cathode ray direction finding equipment. There are four so-called Sferic stations in the UK and they can detect and plot the positions of lightning discharges as far afield as the Mediterranean. Weather radars, which give stronger echoes as the rain or hail becomes more intense, enable thunderstorm areas over sailing waters local to the radars to be detected and followed. You can ask Bracknell the location of any storms that may be breaking out on storm-prone days and such information may be more important to lake and reservoir sailors in the south of Britain than to actual crews going to sea, as most big storms occur over the land with the Home Counties being particularly prone to them. Apart from the special form of thundery disturbances that generate over France and move northwards over the Channel and southern North Sea, the sea areas are remarkably free of major storms. Such statements may not however apply to very storm-prone areas like the Baltic shore of Germany, nor to certain areas of the Mediterranean.

The computer can not tell whether or not thundery conditions are going to obtain in any area. That information comes from the tephigrams that show the state of upper temperature and humidity in the airmass that lies over any region. Here, on some occasions, the radiosonde ascents, coming at 12 hour intervals, leave considerable doubt as to the attributes of an airmass. For thunder to occur widely the upper air must be relatively cold compared with the surface air, but when air subsides from very high levels it warms up. So in the 12 full hours between ascents subsidence may have transformed a thundery upper air into one where clouds are dispersing.

The satellite cloud pictures give another dimension to the real forecast. Through automatic picture transmission (APT) the satellites in orbits that go over the poles (in contrast to geostationary satellites that are permanently over the Equator) automatically transmit their pictures when passing over the Atlantic Europe area (see figure 3.1). The resulting picture of cloud cover, plus snow cover and ice sheets often helps to find or re-position fronts as the wedges of cloud, seen from the ground over a relatively restricted circle of vision, appear on the cloud pictures as swathes of white following the lines of the fronts. Warm fronts will often break into broken skies along their trailing edges and cold fronts along their leading edges. Old depressions which develop large holes in their central cloud cover can be seen actually doing it on the satellite pictures and the forecast for areas still under the sway of the lows can go for partly cloudy or even fair conditions rather than cloudy or even overcast, which was what would have been assumed to be the situation around a depression centre some years ago.

figure 3.1

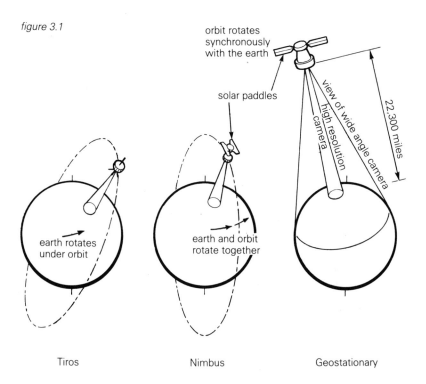

orbit rotates synchronously with the earth

solar paddles

view of wide angle camera

high resolution camera

22,300 miles

earth rotates under orbit

earth and orbit rotate together

Tiros

Nimbus

Geostationary

Satellite orbits. Most satellite pictures displayed on TV are from the modern generation of TIROS satellites. A satellite at 22,300 miles above the Equator rotates in sychronization with the Earth.

The cloud picture is analyzed into cloud type and amount and broadcast in a special code as a nephanalysis (νεφ: Greek, cloud and *nef*: Welsh, heaven). Nephanalyses are a regular feature of fax broadcasts. As well as locating frontal systems and depression centres they show where areas of showers are occurring and so, by continuity of movement, show to where they will migrate in the forecast period.

This form of satellite cloud picture works with visible light (see photograph on page 24). A much more detailed and less distorted picture can be obtained by sensing the infra-red (heat) radiations from all surfaces below the satellite. This is done with a radiometer, which scans the surface below sending out a signal to receivers that makes the coldest object appear bright white and the warmest a shade close to black. Thus the infra-red radiometer picture sees the earth as a sphere varying in temperature and, as temperature is the most important of all weather creating processes, so these pictures are often to be preferred to the more

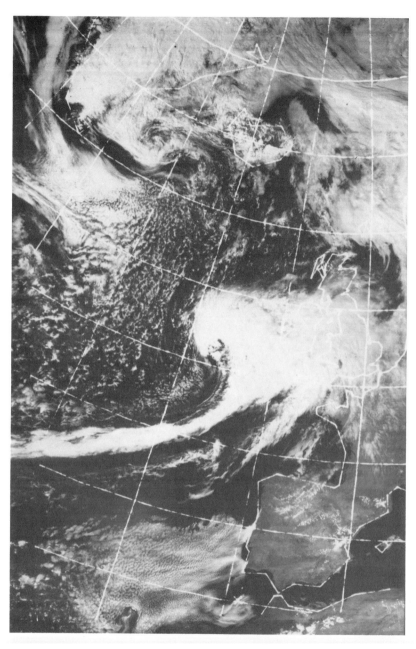

This picture of the eastern Atlantic was taken by TIROS N on its 4290th orbit at 1537 GMT on Monday 13 August 1979. Compare this with fig 1.4. The mass of cloud in the centre is the deepening Fastnet storm. (Photo by courtesy of the University of Dundee Electronics Laboratory.)

conventional visible light ones. Where the land is warm by day the picture will be dark, while the sea surface will be cooler and so lighter. Due to this contrast the coastlines show up sharply in the middle of the summer day. Conversely as visible light is not involved the radiometer pictures come in equally well at night, but now the land will have cooled below the sea temperature and the land masses will be light in colour compared to the surrounding sea areas. The resolution is often sufficient to see warm or cold water regions and so make it more likely that a correct fog forecast will be given in the shipping forecast. Cold clouds appear brightest in the radiometer pictures and so cloud height can be gauged as darker cloud masses must be lower down.

Applications of these techniques of potential use to the mariner include measurement of the roughness of the sea and, on a more long-term scientific level, salinity and sediment distribution as well as the exact position of ocean current limits. The latter could well be of great use to trans-Atlantic racers who may wish either to avoid the currents, or possibly use them when they are favourable to the passage.

One other satellite application can be mentioned and that is the geostationary meteorological satellites that are being put up at set intervals around the Equator and whose low resolution (wide angle) cameras can see the weather from 55°N to 55°S. The one for the European theatre is Meteosat II which is on the Greenwich Meridian at the exact height (about 33,000 km, 17,800 Nmi) where its orbital angular speed is the same as that of the Earth. Thus it remains locked over the latitude and longitude coordinates of 00 (see figure 1.4, page 16). Meteosat II replaced Meteosat I which ceased to function in late 1979. Five such satellites will give full global coverage between the latitudes seen by the cameras and four of them are at present in position. The US has two, one over the Amazon Basin that amongst other things sees the birth and early motion of hurricanes and another over the Eastern Pacific. The Japanese have one over the West Pacific which in its turn will look for the birth of typhoons and their counterparts that not only strike at Japan but occasionally devastate towns in Northern Australia. Satellite pictures will benefit the small craft mariner more and more as time goes by.

All these modern aids help the forecast, but the forecast is still subject to errors and it will be a long time before the techniques substantially improve the overall day-to-day position of the man in the cockpit who will still have to rely on his own interpretations of the forecasts in many nailbiting situations. I can but quote Dr Basil Mason the Director General of the Meteorological Office; in his 'state of the service' broadcast in 1978 he remarked that the British met effort stands comparison with any other in the world, but added that 'the major problems of meteorology are still unsolved'. That may seem a little harsh, but it shows how meteorologists view their craft. They know that they often have to work from hand-to-mouth and frequently hunch plays a considerable part in the details of forecasts. The fact is that often it is not the weather that fails to follow form, it is the time at which it arrives over you that is wrong. It will be a long and laborious uphill struggle to truly improve the forecast in its statement of when, rather than what. This is particularly true of fronts which develop waves and slow down without warning. So the small craft mariner watching his own patch of sky can do a great deal to improve the forecast for his own area.

4 Finding the forecasts

However much met knowledge you acquire over the years, no one with any sense puts to sea without a forecast. Despite certain spectacular and easily remembered lapses on the part of the forecast services there is no doubt that forecasts are getting better. The general inferences on the state of the weather for the next couple of days, which are now given on a routine basis with broadcast forecasts, are vastly more right than wrong. What may not commend the professionals to the crew of sailing yachts is how they cannot very often get the wind right for your bit of water; this is what the yachtsman has to do for himself. There is no other sport where every nuance of the wind is so important or so noticeable and the met services are not geared to giving the kind of detail that most sailing people would like.

What you need to do when you read, hear or see a forecast is to use it as a guide to the major wind direction to be expected, but you must modify it for your own time of day and position. No forecast service will be able to provide a sufficiently detailed pattern of the wind to always please the crew of the yacht that say leaves an English Channel port for France or an East Anglian haven for the Dutch coast. Although you can ask for personal forecasts to be sent to you for a passage by telephone at a pre-arranged time or by telegram, very few avail themselves of such a service because of its inherent difficulties and its cost. More likely they listen to a radio forecast or look at the TV weather map. The table below lists most of the methods available.

Means of obtaining forecasts
RADIO
a National broadcasts
Highly important coverage because high powered (long wave) transmitters reach most areas to which people cruise. For example, BBC on 1500 m

(200 kHz) is the listening station for gale warnings in English. <u>France</u> <u>Inter (Allouis) on 1829 m (164 kHz) is similar in French etc (see</u> appendix). Also on medium wave transmitters

Forecasts for shipping, coastal waters and land areas come out at set times of day. There is no coverage during the later watches of the night. Important because everyone has a domestic receiver on which to pick up the forecasts and listen out for gales (see appendix). The range of coverage from the high powered transmitters is vast – way out into the Atlantic and over most of the coasts of Atlantic Europe. France's station is designed to reach the Mediterranean including North Africa

b Local broadcasting

This is truly local being on limited range medium wave transmitters and on VHF. However these stations often give best coverage for their own area

Local radio stations both national and commercial often cover their local waters in great detail, giving tide times and special summertime forecasts for water sports of all kinds. Ring local stations along a cruising route to see what is available

c Marine radio

Two way communication on marine band VHF radio to coast radio stations and to coastguards

Any serious cruising person should invest in a two-way marine radio. It is a very comforting thing to have about. Consult the bigger chandlers about the best one for your requirements

d Radio facsimile

Charts, synopses, prognoses etc via a special facsimile receiver. Can be an adjunct to your own marine receiver

Not yet fully off the ground but when it is this will keep the latest met information rolling off the machine. Your only problem will then be to interpret the charts etc. If you intend to go far south where forecasts are only in French or Spanish consider installing a lightweight fax

TELEVISION

e National broadcasts

The way that most people get a sight of the latest chart

The weathercasters usually come on following major newscasts and times are in newspapers and *TV* and *Radio Times*. Nearly all stations give a weathercast during their magazine programmes around six in the evening. See page 99 for special symbols used on BBC TV

f Local TV

Wide divergence from region to region but when good these may be the best way of assessing the prospects

Local TV weathercasts vary greatly in coverage but the trend is to show more charts and employ a forecast team to deliver them. Occasionally the local sage is called in to pronounce some weather lore – such gimmickry is best avoided

g *Viewdata*
Forecasts at regular intervals on special 'pages' using adapted TV receivers or, as with Prestel in Britain, using telephone landlines and special TV receivers

If installing a new TV attempt to get one modified for the reception of Viewdata pages. Constantly updated weather forecasts are given as routine, but the method of presentation will not allow charts to be drawn. More and better information is obtained on special PO Prestel receivers to obtain a greatly enhanced source of information including coastal waters' forecasts

TELEPHONE
h *Pre-recorded forecasts*
Good local coverage specially, in many cases, for coastal areas

For the quick do-I-go-or-not appraisal this service is amongst the best. Always there and constantly updated the information is for a limited coastal area and so is more precise. Available widely in Atlantic and Mediterranean France plus other European countries

j *Public service met stations*
Personal forecasts and information, man to man. Best for answering specific questions

If the above is not specific enough this is the service which will expand your knowledge of the weather as seen through the eyes of a forecaster on the spot

k *Coastguard*
For actual local weather plus the official forecast in force at the time

Coastguards will not do any forecasting off their own bat. They are restricted to the actual weather they can see or is reported to them by their cutters etc. The forecast they have is the same official one that is on the radio or the pre-recorded telephone

PRINTED
m *Newspapers*
Inevitably rather old forecasts plus, in some cases, actual or forecast charts

Useful if no other more-up-to-date source is available. Can be pondered and imbibed on the way home from the office before a weekend or longer afloat. Always re-check what the paper says with one of the other more easily modified channels of information

n Windows of weather shops
Weather shops are few and far between, but good if you happen to pass by on the way from the office and can stop to look at the charts or call in for information. They are amongst the best centres to ring for personal forecasts
In the centres of large cities

5 Forecasts for sea areas

All countries with coastlines provide their own forecasts for shipping, which is not the same as saying they provide an adequate service for yachts. Merchantmen and small craft share the same fog risk, but they do not share the same gale risk. Very few ships are at risk with winds below Force 7–8, but most yachts are seeking shelter before it gets to Force 7. Only a few weather services give strong wind warnings so that rarely are winds of Force 6 or 7 included in gale warnings.

Until recently this was the case in this country and when I sat down to write this book I was lamenting the fact (as so many of us had for so many years) that Force 8 was still the gale criterion for warnings. However it is good to be able to include here the details of what are known as Small Craft Warnings which are now issued by the Met Office whenever winds of Force 6 or more are expected within the next 12 hours. Almost all the radio stations local to the coast, whether BBC or IBA, are participants in the scheme and the warnings of Force 6 or more in the five mile strip adjacent to the coast are given at the first programme juncture and repeated on the next hour or after a newscast. However this is only a 'summer service' from Easter until the end of October and outside these dates the met service will still use Force 8 as its criterion for issuing gale warnings leaving small craft to interpret their situation as best they can. Thus over the winter period it is important to find out if gale warnings are in force for sea areas adjacent to your own, because even if the wind is not expected to rise to Force 8 in your area, it could well rise to Force 6 and so constitute a yacht gale on the periphery of the main blow.

The sea areas are all differently drawn by the major countries so the sea area map (figure 5.1) is of the British areas. How their basic designations vary and their names in other languages are given in the appendix for the sea areas surrounding the British Isles. Often a certain nation's sea area spans two or more of the ones chosen as basic. In this case the same name

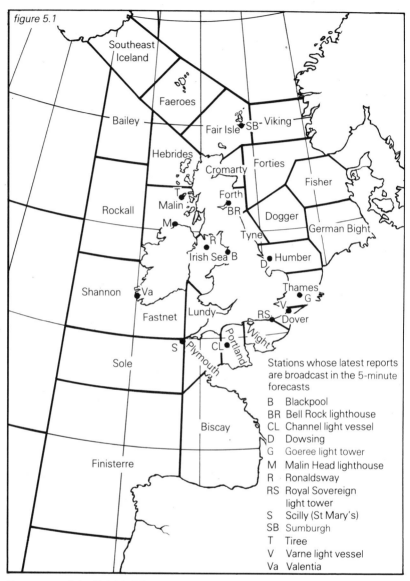

Figure caption and legend within image:

> figure 5.1

Stations whose latest reports are broadcast in the 5-minute forecasts

B   Blackpool
BR   Bell Rock lighthouse
CL   Channel light vessel
D   Dowsing
G   Goeree light tower
M   Malin Head lighthouse
R   Ronaldsway
RS   Royal Sovereign light tower
S   Scilly (St Mary's)
SB   Sumburgh
T   Tiree
V   Varne light vessel
Va   Valentia

Sea areas of the British Isles.

will appear in two areas. The limits of areas are purely arbitrary and weather knows no bounds so a forecast for a certain sea area can easily spill across the divisions into others. Hence the exact delineation of each country's areas has not been considered necessary. Belgium uses exactly the same sea areas as Britain.

It must be remembered that the elements used in shipping forecasts are

30

directed at big ships; the policy with regard to the broadcasting of shipping forecasts is dictated by the big shipping companies and the yachtsman's voice on this is small even if it is vociferous. Times of forecasts are tailored to the watch system at sea which are often not the best times for small craft crews. Strict time limits are usually set on the radio shipping forecasts by the broadcasting companies and in this country the exact five minutes is often adhered to religiously, however complex the situation may be, so that possibly vital actuals are left off the end of the delivery. Other countries may well be better off in this respect and it will be seen from figure 5.2 that most of the coasts of Europe north of the Channel give their forecasts in English as well as their own tongue so making English the international working language. France gives its forecasts only in French and Spain broadcasts only in Spanish (see figure 5.3). The Portuguese station of Monsanto however does give storm warnings in English, but they are on WT and not RT, so are not of great use to most yachts. Thus we can say that north of 50°N you can go anywhere with English, but south of it you will need the host country's language. It has therefore only seemed necessary to add important weather phrases in French and Spanish as an appendix (see page 199).

The importance of gale warnings is appreciated by all radio services that deal with them and they will in general be broadcast as soon after receipt as practicable. In Britain BBC Radio 4 is the 'gale' station and in the Netherlands it is Hilversum 3. Not all countries broadcast gale warnings on receipt using a long wave high power transmitter.

The very real differences between deep water weather and inshore water weather is not adequately recognized in shipping forecasts and so when a shipping forecast is heard the yachtsman planning to sail inshore waters must modify the situation outlined in the forecast to take account of his position. If the wind is off-shore (in this book off-shore is used to mean 'from shoreward', and offshore means 'deeper waters'; on-shore means 'from seaward') then he has shelter and the weather of the land mass, but if the wind is on-shore then he is on a lee shore, coastal shallows will heap up seas that will not be found in deeper water, but the wind will have an 'oceanic' fetch and so will the seaway. In more pleasant conditions of light winds the coastal waters will by day develop seabreeze regimes which will bear no relation to the wind directions forecast for offshore sea areas, or they may say something vague like 'light, variable' which leaves you entirely on your own as the light and variable wind is the one under which you have to make passage.

Overleaf: Radio transmitters which give gale warnings in the main home cruising waters.

figure 5.2

Orkney
Ch 26 (Wick)

Lewis Ch 5

Wick (GKR)
1827 kHz

Skye Ch 24

Cromarty
Ch 28 (Wick)

Stonehaven (GND
1856 kHz Ch 26

Oban (GNE)
2740 kHz

Forth Ch 24
(Stonehaven

55°N

Islay
Ch 25

Portpatrick (GPK)
1883 kHz Ch 27

Anglesey (GLV)
1715 kHz Ch 26

R T Eireann
566 kHz

Valentia (EJK)
1827 kHz

Celtic Ch 24

Severn Ch 25

Ilfracombe (GIL)
2670 kHz

50°N

Start
Ch 26

Lands End (GLD)
1841 kHz Ch 27

Jersey (GUD
1726 kHz

Brest (FFU)
1806 kHz

Radio Fra
Rennes 7

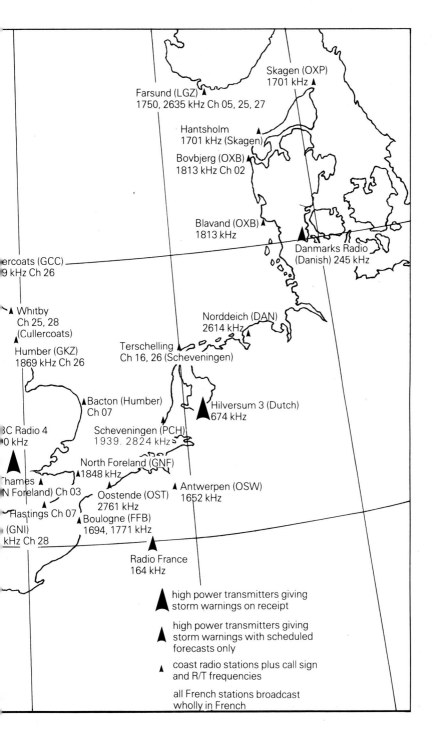

Skagen (OXP)
1701 kHz ▲

Farsund (LGZ) ▲
1750, 2635 kHz Ch 05, 25, 27

Hantsholm
1701 kHz (Skagen) ▲

Bovbjerg (OXB) ▲
1813 kHz Ch 02

Blavand (OXB) ▲
1813 kHz

Danmarks Radio
(Danish) 245 kHz

ercoats (GCC)
9 kHz Ch 26

▲ Whitby
Ch 25, 28
(Cullercoats)

Norddeich (DAN)
2614 kHz ▲

Humber (GKZ)
1869 kHz Ch 26

Terschelling ▲
Ch 16, 26 (Scheveningen)

▲ Bacton (Humber)
Ch 07

Hilversum 3 (Dutch)
674 kHz

3C Radio 4
0 kHz

Scheveningen (PCH)
1939. 2824 kHz

North Foreland (GNF)
▲ 1848 kHz

Thames ▲
N Foreland) Ch 03

Oostende (OST)
2761 kHz

▲ Antwerpen (OSW)
1652 kHz

Hastings Ch 07
(GNI)
kHz Ch 28

▲ Boulogne (FFB)
1694, 1771 kHz

Radio France
164 kHz

▲ high power transmitters giving
storm warnings on receipt

▲ high power transmitters giving
storm warnings with scheduled
forecasts only

▲ coast radio stations plus call sign
and R/T frequencies

all French stations broadcast
wholly in French

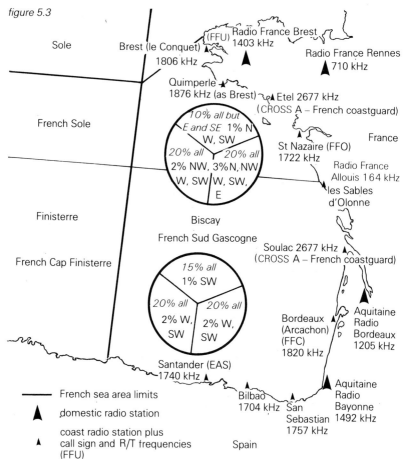

figure 5.3

Met services on the Atlantique coast of France. To interpret the wind roses, see figure 10.1.

Gale Stations

When cruising round Britain and in the North Sea you are always in radio range of the BBC Radio 4 high power transmitter on 200 kHz. The Athlone transmitter of Radio Telefis Eireann is of lower power, but also gives gale warnings on receipt. On the Continental side only Hilversum 3 gives gale warnings on receipt in Dutch. Unless otherwise stated all the coast radio stations shown give plain language warnings and forecasts in English. Gale warnings are given after first silence period and forecasts are usually on a four or six hourly schedule. A resumé of the Coast Radio Stations that broadcast in English is to be found in the appendix. For full details see the *Admiralty List of Radio Signals Volume III* with which you need supplement 283a showing the forecast areas. For a synopsis see either the RYA booklet 'Weather Forecasts' or a nautical almanac.

In the diagrams of the radio stations from which gale and other warnings can be obtained all stations broadcast in English and the home language with notable exceptions. French stations broadcast wholly in French (see page 199), German domestic radio has not been included as it does not give gale warnings on receipt. To convert frequencies in kilohertz (kHz) into wavelength in metres divide the frequency into 300,000 eg BBC Radio 4 has a wavelength of 300,000/200 = 1500 metres.

6 Forecasts for land areas

For small craft use the local land area forecasts are of the highest value because the majority of cruising yachts do not habitually go out of sight of the land. Coastwise or coastal weather is mainly land weather, and not sea weather at all. Only when the wind is blowing from the sea with a good fetch is the coastal weather typical of deep water areas as given in the shipping forecasts. In any case shipping forecasts are sparse and inconveniently timed, and most people turn to the early morning land area forecasts for a statement of the likely conditions during the coming day. For sailing, the forecasts as given need reinforcing by a good measure of local knowledge and experience, and if you have specific questions to ask it is best to ring a Weather Information Office and speak to a forecaster.

The areas into which Great Britain and Eire are divided for forecast purposes are shown in figure 6.1, and these also include the numbers used by the newspapers to identify the regions. Weather centres are specifically set up to serve the public as a first priority and within reason provide a service 24 hours a day, seven days a week. These and other main public service offices are located on the map in the appendix. They are the centres to ring when you want a run-down on the current situation and an idea of how things will develop. The computed prognoses now allow some guidance to be given out to three days ahead and an extension to six days is in being, however it would be wise to take such 'long-range' forecasts with a certain pinch of salt and keep a careful eye on how the situation develops in the short term.

The following words are used to identify statements on the weather:

A weather 'report' is of actual weather that existed, ie you are being given an observation or a set of observations from some specific place or places at some time in the immediate past. If, for example, you want to know what the weather was recently at Spurn Point ask for a report.

A weather 'forecast' is a statement of future trends for a given locality.

figure 6.1

28 Shetland

27 Orkney

24 NE Scotland

23 Moray Firth area

NW Scotland. 26

19 Aberdeen area

Central Highlands
22

Argyll 25

18 Edinburgh and Dundee areas

Glasgow area
21

17 Borders

Eire Northwest

29
N Ireland

SW Scotland
20

16 NE England

Eire Northeast

13
Lake District

Eire
West

Eire
Midlands

Eire
East

14
Isle of Man

NW England 12

Central
N England
15

6 East England

11

North Wales

Eire
Southeast

7
Midlands
West

5
Midlands
East

3 East Anglia

Eire
Southwest

Eire
South

10
South Wales

1 Greater London

4 Central
S England

2 SE England

9 SW England

Channel Islands 8

A weather 'warning' notifies the expected onset of gales, thunderstorms, fog, frost and snow in the near future for a stated locality or localities.

It must be borne in mind that the two most important elements of any coastwise forecast, wind speed and the likelihood of sea fog, will not normally be covered by land area forecasts. The wind speed at sea may well be two Beaufort forces above the suggested force ashore when the wind is blowing from the land to the sea (see page 72). This is especially so at night where the wind can be 5 knots ashore in the early hours and 15–20 knots offshore. The development of sea fog is often a case of having enough sea fetch to humidify and cool the air so that a windward coast is fog free, but a leeward coast is covered.

7 Forecasts by telephone

For a quick local forecast for a specific area, which is available throughout the 24 hours, there is nothing to beat pre-recorded telephone forecasts. They are always there and are updated several times a day. They give a general synopsis, the weather expected, temperature, wind and an outlook for the following 24 hours. Their numbers can be looked up in the Telephone Information Services pages at the front of the Directory.

If you want more detailed information then ring a Weather Information Office whose numbers will also be found under Telephone Information Services in the phone book. Ask to speak to the forecaster and if possible have an idea of what the situation looks like already so that you can ask precise and specific questions. If you know which lows, highs and fronts are on the chart then you and he will be speaking the same language and you will get the benefit of the professional's feeling that he is speaking to someone who is on the ball and has done some homework.

Some meteorological offices do not work a 24-hour day, so if you ring in the evening or early morning you may be told that there is no forecaster on duty. You will be talking to a met assistant who is not allowed to give forecasts off his own bat. He can however give you actual weather, can read observations off the teleprinter and may quote the guidance synopses that come to the office from the Central Forecasting Office via the facsimile machine.

In addition to these free services you may ask for a tailormade forecast for your regatta day or big race. This can be requested at any time in

Names of regions mentioned in British domestic weather forecasts.

advance of the day, but again be specific as to the elements you want to appear in the forecast. In addition you can make arrangements to have gale warnings for your own or any area phoned through to you during any specified period, or if necessary, whenever a gale is forecast for your local area. You can ask for a weekend forecast to be phoned through on a Friday evening to your home or the club, but again ask for exactly what you require or it may become long and costly.

A less well-known telephone service, useful for important events, is the Telecopier, which is a form of facsimile machine designed to be used with your own telephone line. There are three authorities to be contacted for this service. The Post Office will arrange to fit a jack socket to the phone you intend to use, but the Telecopier has to be hired (or bought) from the company who makes them (names in this field are Rank Xerox and Interscandex). Lastly and most importantly the Meteorological Office must be approached for advice on what it can deliver and what you actually require. However here is a way to get up-to-date and specific forecasts and weather charts to go with them for important race briefings etc. The service may however prove to be fairly expensive as the Post Office charge the time at normal telephone call rates, the telecopier company charge for the hire and the Met Office charge for the time to prepare forecasts and charts and also for handling the material you require. With this in mind a Committee might consider the ongoing advantages of their own fax machine using airwave broadcasts which, while not specifically tailored for their purposes, will at least provide an ever-present source of charts and forecasts (see page 41).

France divides its coastline into 'Manche et Atlantique' and 'Mediterranée' and has automatic recorded telephone forecast facilities for Dunkerque, Boulogne, Le Havre, Caen, Cherbourg, Granville, Dinard, Bréhat, Morlaix, Brest, Lorient, Rennes, Nantes, la Roche sur Yon, La Rochelle, Royan, Arcachon and Biarritz on the first length of coastline and at Canet-Plage, Perpignan, La Grande Motte, Cap d'Agde, Leucate, St Cyprien, Montpelier, Marseille, Marignane, Toulon, St Tropez, Nice, Ajaccio and Bastia in the Mediterranean. All these forecasts are solely in French.

Other countries bordering the North Sea do not have similar prerecorded forecast facilities but provide, like all countries, advice, which may be in English, from selected met stations and airfields. All such information will be found in the telephone directories of the host country which of course entails going ashore and being prepared to at least ask for the facility required in the vernacular.

8 The role of the coastguard

The great friend of the coastwise sailor is the coastguard and it is the first thought of the majority of skippers to ask the coastguard what conditions are like before they sail. It obviously helps to have made an on-the-spot check of what the sea conditions are like before you venture out. However that is where the weather role of the coastguard stops – at actual weather conditions. Coastguards will not forecast the weather – it is not their job – but they will be in touch with a great deal of local weather information and can quote you the shipping forecast which they either take down from the radio just as you would, or they may have a telex/facsimile link to the Met Office.

The coastguard service has recently been reorganized (see figure 8.1) into six search and rescue regions (SRR's). Each region is overseen by a marine rescue coordination centre (MRCC) whose locations will be found on the map below. In addition 22 of what used to be known as rescue headquarters have been re-designated maritime rescue sub-centres (MRSC). Some of this reorganizational thinking surrounds the coastguard's role in preventing pollution at sea, but it also becomes more

The main coastguard centres around the coasts of Britain and Eire.

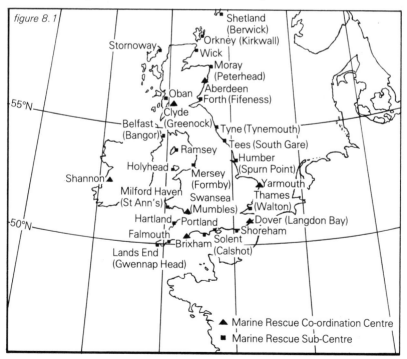

figure 8.1

Shetland (Berwick)
Orkney (Kirkwall)
Stornoway
Wick
Moray (Peterhead)
Aberdeen
Forth (Fifeness)
Oban
55°N
Clyde
Belfast (Greenock)
(Bangor)
Tyne (Tynemouth)
Ramsey
Tees (South Gare)
Holyhead
Humber (Spurn Point)
Shannon
Mersey (Formby)
Milford Haven
Yarmouth
(St Ann's)
Thames
Swansea (Walton)
(Mumbles)
50°N
Hartland Portland
Dover (Langdon Bay)
Falmouth
Shoreham
Brixham
Solent
Lands End
(Calshot)
(Gwennap Head)

▲ Marine Rescue Co-ordination Centre
■ Marine Rescue Sub-Centre

necessary as the sophistication of equipment grows. For better or for worse the number of constantly manned coastguard stations round the coast has been decreased. Thus the letters CG on the chart no longer automatically mean that a coastguard station exists or if it exists, that it is manned.

However, using the current official forecast as a basis, and with the information from local lightvessels, other ships and its own auxiliary coastguards afloat etc the coastguard at one of the 28 rescue centres is in a very good position to give real guidance on the expected conditions and, with their capability to draw on air-sea rescue facilities direct, it is best to ring one of these centres rather than a more local day-watch centre. This does not apply however when conditions threaten to be foggy, as with patchy fog it may be as bright as a button within the local compass of the rescue centre and yet totally obscured further down the coast. In this case the day-watch centres have a role to play just as they have when planning a simple out-and-back fishing or other short trip.

It is worth drawing attention to the Coastguard Yacht and Boat Safety Scheme which is designed to help mount a successful search and rescue operation for you, should you be overdue or need assistance. The boat owner fills in a reply-paid card with details of the craft, its life raft or dinghy, the type of radio it carries and its habitual movements. This is retained at one of the 28 rescue headquarters nearest to your home base, while a shore contact's name, address and telephone number enables the coastguard to contact someone who knows about you. This contact also has a portion of the card with the Coastguard Rescue Headquarters name and number deposited with him.

Weather Safety at Sea

Before you go to sea get a reliable forecast.

Compare the forecast's statement of immediate weather prospects with the weather you have. If the two differ radically find out why.

Tell the coastguard when you hope to sail and where you hope to get to.

Always carry adequate lifesaving equipment for all the crew and see it is regularly serviced.

Have a VHF radio so you can call the coastguard direct on Channel 16 if you have a distress or emergency call. If you wish to report position or a change of plan still call on Channel 16 stating you have 'safety traffic' then switch to CH 67 (a special safety channel between coastguard and small craft) to give your message.

If outside VHF range contact a coast radio station on MF radio periodically to report your 'TR' (a TR is a position report).

9 Facsimile

This is an increasingly important means by which anyone with the right equipment can receive up-to-date plotted charts using the whole resources of the met communications network.

Fax (which is not to be confused with viewdata systems like Ceefax and Oracle) can be received by landline (telephone facsimile) or via airwave broadcasting (radio fascimile). In either case a special chart drawing machine is required. In the past the machines available were quite impracticable for use at sea on yachts, although many are to be found in the chartrooms of the merchant fleet and the navy. Today an increasing number of light facsimile recorders are coming on to the market aimed at the small craft market and that market can be potentially large, so that although the equipment may seem costly at present it is likely to come down with time and when this happens more and more sail and power yachts will fit it (see photograph on page 42).

The potential usefulness of a fax recorder on a yacht at sea is immense and only limited by the ability of the recipient to interpret the advanced weather information it can provide. A typical receiver occupies a space of 1½ ft × 1½ ft × 9 in, and weighs in the region of 11 or 12 pounds (5 kg). It draws charts on the size of about A4 paper, ie about 8 in (200 mm) wide and a roll of the special paper contains about 200 ft (60 m). That means something over 150 charts etc per roll allowing for gaps in the broadcasting schedule.

The facsimile transmitters cover all the areas to which European yachts normally sail and Europe has the highest density of stations. Each major country considers it important to have its own facsimile output and each one provides localized information for its own waters that the others do not. The worldwide network of stations is shown in figure 9.1.

The major countries of Europe including the Parisian stations of Ste.Assise and Pintoise, broadcast facsimile; Madrid comes in with surface analyses, satellite data and wave prognoses. The American backed Rota station (also in Spain) gives a very wide coverage and its schedules are re-broadcast from Thurso and Londonderry in the UK as well as from Morocco and Nea Makri in Greece. The fax station in Germany is Quickborn/Pinneberg and Moscow includes charts of most of the northern hemisphere, plus wave height analyses and satellite cloud data from the Tropics and the southern hemisphere. Helsinki gives ice charts and sea surface temperatures for its waters as well as forecast charts. Stockholm does the same, and it is obvious that most European countries contribute to the 'instant chart' revolution. All that is required is sufficient market interest to lower the price and improve the reliability of the 'domestic'

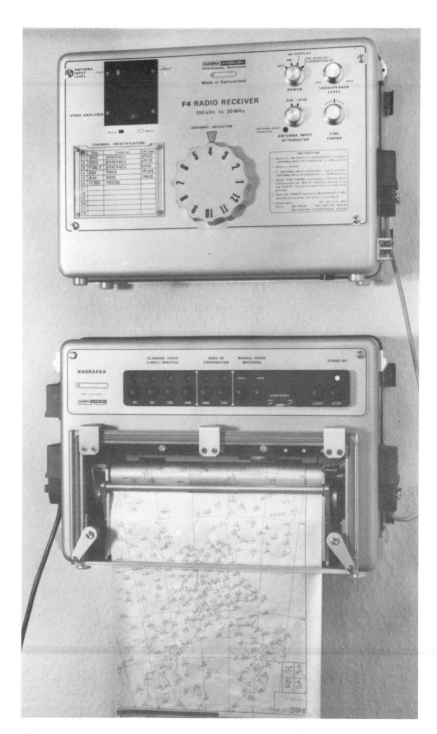

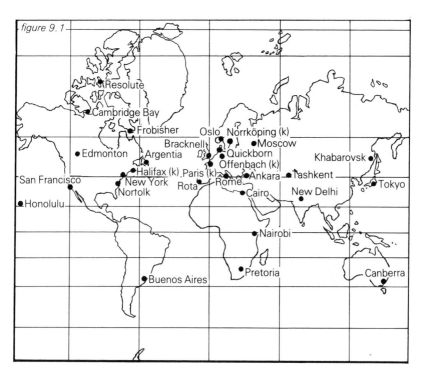

figure 9.1

Resolute
Cambridge Bay
Frobisher
Oslo Norrköping (k)
Bracknell
Moscow
Edmonton
Argentia
Quickborn
Khabarovsk
Offenbach (k)
San Francisco
Halifax (k)
Paris (k)
Ankara
Tashkent
New York
Rota
Rome
Tokyo
Norfolk
Cairo
New Delhi
Honolulu
Nairobi
Buenos Aires
Pretoria
Canberra

The major facsimile stations of the world. Most broadcast in the decametric range but those marked (k) broadcast in the kilometric range and are often of high power.

machines and everyone will want one. A typical schedule of facsimile output will include:

Surface charts (analyses) for the North Atlantic Area for 0000, 0600, 1200 and 1800
Forecast charts for the same area for 24 hours ahead (prognoses)
Forecast surface charts for up to three days ahead
Wave analyses and forecasts for up to 48 hours ahead
Analyzed versions of the satellite cloud pictures (nephanalyses)

Because of the universal language of weather symbols and methods, the reception of facsimile charts from foreign stations still allows the recipient who has little or no knowledge of the host language to use effectively the

A lightweight fax receiver using metallic sensitized paper designed for use in yachts. It has its own decametric receiver suitable for the reception of the output from most of the world's facsimile stations. (Photo by courtesy of Nagra, Cheseaux sur Lausanne, Switzerland.)

fax output of the whole of Europe. In practice the British yachtsman may well find himself tuning to Paris or Quickborn (near Hamburg) for his Channel, North Sea and Baltic information. This is because the fax broadcasts from Bracknell (for merchantmen) and Northwood (for the fleet) are mainly concerned with the Atlantic Ocean and the resultant charts are on rather a small scale when reproduced on domestic fax equipment. Continental stations being further from the open ocean tend to consider ships that have to sail the more enclosed waters before they reach the open sea. Thus their output, while not aimed in any way at small craft, tends to be of more use to yachts.

Some technical details might be useful here. The 'Index of Cooperation' is the ratio of the scanning speed and the paper feed speed – either 576 or half that (288) – and this value is quoted with the schedules in the *Admiralty List of Radio Signals Volume III (ALRS III)*. The scanning (or drum) speed of all important European fax broadcasts is 120 rpm and the two figures appear alongside the details of the schedule as 120/576 or 120/288. Very occasionally another scanning speed is used, but of the major originators only Moskva departs seriously from the above.

10 Gales

Despite the vast mass of yachts and the fact that the sum total of their crew members far and away outstrips the numbers of their merchant navy colleagues, gale warnings in shipping forecasts are for big ships and not for small ones. Thus, 'Gale Force 8 imminent' is what you expect to hear and not 'Yacht Gale Force 6 imminent' as you might like.

You have to allow for the fact that most gales do rise at a more-or-less steady rate and so when a gale warning is issued for your sea area it will rise to what, for you, may be dangerous proportions (or already have assumed those proportions) sooner than the words describing the forecast period would suggest. Thus a Force 8 gale 'soon' can mean a Force 6 'gale' is imminent and may mean Force 6 *now*. So the yacht crew offshore have to monitor the gale warnings for sea areas close to their own as well as the one they happen to be in and listen out for Small Craft Warnings for coastal regions from local radio stations.

Gales grow when lows and highs come into too close proximity and neither will give way; then the isobars tighten and the wind climbs fast. It is therefore more likely that gales will occur far from a depression centre rather than close to it. Likewise the edges of anticyclones are where the wind may become strongest and stay that way for some considerable time.

Because depressions deepen and anticyclones tend to resist changing their pressure, the number of isobars between a low and a high centre has to increase with time and that means an increase in wind.

Thus situations where a high or ridge has been established for many days are ones prone to strong winds when depressions from the Atlantic start tilting at the dominance of the high; gales from the south or southwest often result in the west due to this. Or the Azores high stretches a ridge across Biscay and into France while deep lows run across Scotland and into Scandinavia. Each low brings strong westerlies across southern and central Britain and so across the North Sea as well.

Gales may come from many directions depending on the locality, but the direction most favoured is S or SW. In figure 10.1 the major gale directions for selected localities around the cruising grounds of Atlantic Europe are shown.

As already pointed out yachts at sea should monitor BBC Radio 4 on 1500 m (200 kHz) for the first indications of gales and note when they are forecast for sea areas local to their own, but not necessarily in it. Expect the wind in your area to rise to Force 6 if there are Force 8 warnings out for an adjacent one. Also allow for the fact that sometimes the state of the atmosphere is such that it permits a corridor of strong wind to build down say the North Sea or up the Channel when peripheral areas only have fresh winds.

There are some areas more prone to gales than others. Gales in the Channel are fewer than they are in the North Sea and there the most gale-prone area is perhaps the coastal waters of the Low Countries. In this connection the Dutch station of Scheviningen broadcasts gale warnings on receipt in English as well as Dutch for Force 7 and above plus giving a forecast four times a day for its coastal waters and the North Sea generally, plus the Ijsselmeer. It also gives very useful actual weather reports from local stations (for frequencies and times see the appendix).

Gale Warnings

The following are the criteria on which gale warnings are issued:

	mean wind speed	highest gust speed
Gale warning	Force 8	43 knots
Severe gale	Force 9	52 knots
Storm	Force 10	61 knots

Overleaf: Gale frequencies in the cruising areas around Britain through the three seasons.

45

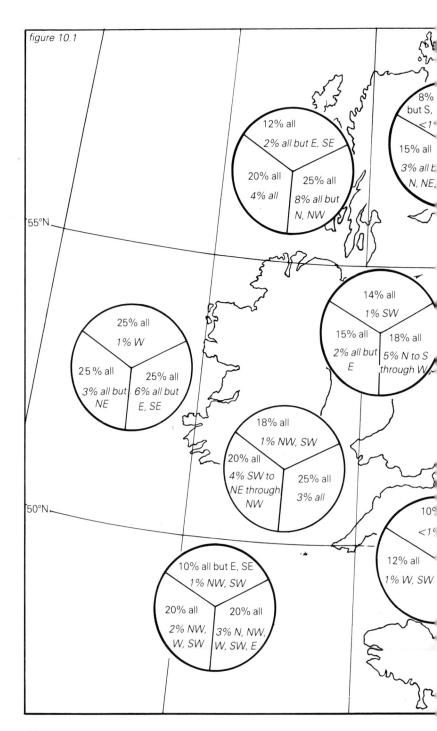

figure 10.1

12% all
2% all but E, SE
20% all
4% all
25% all
8% all but N, NW

8%
but S,
<1
15% all
3% all b
N, NE,

14% all
1% SW
15% all
2% all but E
18% all
5% N to S through W

25% all
1% W
25% all
3% all but NE
25% all
6% all but E, SE

18% all
1% NW, SW
20% all
4% SW to NE through NW
25% all
3% all

10
<1
12% all
1% W, SW

10% all but E, SE
1% NW, SW
20% all
2% NW, W, SW
20% all
3% N, NW, W, SW, E

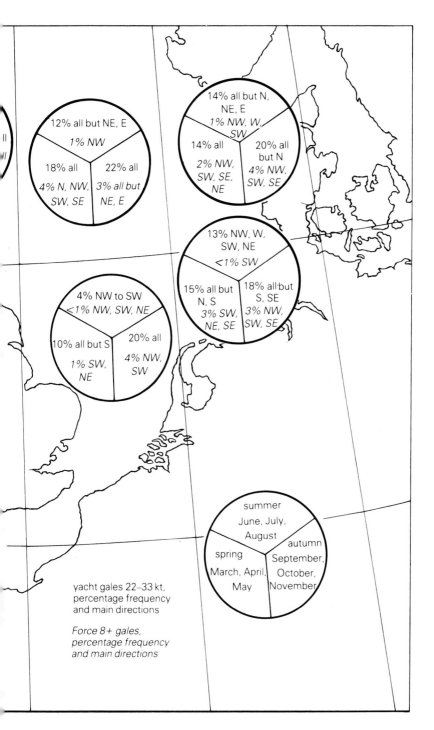

12% all but NE, E
1% NW
18% all   22% all
4% N, NW,   3% all but
SW, SE   NE, E

14% all but N, NE, E
1% NW, W, SW
14% all   20% all but N
2% NW, SW, SE, NE   4% NW, SW, SE

13% NW, W, SW, NE
<1% SW
15% all but N, S   18% all but S, SE
3% SW, NE, SE   3% NW, SW, SE

4% NW to SW
<1% NW, SW, NE
10% all but S   20% all
1% SW, NE   4% NW, SW

summer
June, July, August
spring   autumn
March, April, May   September, October, November

yacht gales 22–33 kt,
percentage frequency
and main directions

*Force 8+ gales,
percentage frequency
and main directions*

Description of wind strength in sea area forecasts (Beaufort Scale)

Beaufort number	General description	Limit of mean speed (knots)	Land signs	Dinghy criteria	Deep keel criteria	State of sea (see section 12 for details)
0	Calm	less than 1	Smoke rises vertically. Leaves do not stir	Sails will not fill. Racing flag will not respond. Flies and tell tails might just respond	Boom swings idly in the swell. Racing flags and anemometers will not respond. Flies and tell tails might just	Sea mirror-smooth. Calm enough to preserve shape of reflections of sails, masts etc.
1	Light air	1 to 3	Smoke drifts. Wind vanes do not respond	Sails fill. Racing flag may not be reliable. Flies and tell tails respond. Crew and helmsman on opposite sides of craft	Sails just fill, but little way made. Racing flags and vanes may respond but cup anemometers may not. Flies and tell tails respond. Spinnakers do not fill	Scaly or shell-shaped ripples. No foam crests to be seen on open sea
2	Light breeze	4 to 6	Wind felt on the face. Leaves rustle. Light flags not extended. Wind vanes respond	Useful way can be made. Racing flag reliable. Helmsman and crew both sit to windward. Spinnakers may fill	Wind felt on the cheek. Controlled way made. Spinnakers and sails generally fill. Racing flags and anemometers respond and are reliable	Small short wavelets with glassy crests that do not break
3	Gentle breeze	7 to 10	Light flags extended. Leaves in constant motion	Helmsman and crew sit on weather gunwale. Spinnakers fill. Fourteen-footers and above may plane	Good way made. Light flags fully extended	Large wavelets. Crests may break but foam is of glassy appearance. A few scattered white horses may be seen when wind at upper limit
4	Moderate breeze	11 to 16	Most flags extend fully. Small branches move. Dust and loose paper may be raised	Dinghy crews lie out. Twelve-foot dinghies may plane: longer dinghies will plane. The best general working breeze	Best general working breeze for all craft. Genoas at optimum	Small waves lengthen. Fairly frequent white horses
5	Fresh breeze	17 to 21	Small trees in leaf sway. Tops of tall trees in noticeable motion	Dinghies ease sheets in gusts. Crews use all weight to keep craft upright. Genoas near	Craft's way somewhat impeded by seaway. Genoas near their limit. Spinnakers still carried	Moderate waves. Many white horses

Beaufort number	General description	Limit of mean speed (knots)	Land signs	Dinghy criteria	Deep keel criteria	State of sea (see section 12 for details)
6	Strong breeze	22 to 27	Large branches in motion. Whistling heard in wires	Dinghies overpowered when carrying full sail. Many capsizes. Crews find difficulty in holding craft upright even when spilling wind	Edge of 'yacht gale' force. Cruising craft seek shelter. Reefing recommended to meet gusts when cruising	Large waves form and extensive foam crests are prevalent. Spray may be blown off some wave tops
7	Near gale (American usage: Moderate gale)	28 to 33	Whole trees in motion. Inconvenience felt when walking against wind	Dinghies fully reefed. Difficult to sail even on main alone. This is the absolute top limit for dinghies — other than in extremis	Yacht gale force when most cruising craft seek shelter. Racing yachts may just carry spinnakers. Reefing essential	Sea heaps up and white foam from breaking waves begins to be blown in streaks along the wind direction
8	Gale (Fresh gale)	34 to 40	Twigs broken off trees. Generally impeded progress on foot. Rarely experienced inland	Dinghies may survive if expertly handled in the seaway on foresail alone	Gale force in anybody's language. Only necessity or ocean racing keeps craft at sea. Set storm canvas or heave-to	Moderately high waves of greater length. Edges of crests begin to break into spindrift. Foam blown in well-marked streaks along the wind
9	Strong gale (Strong gale)	41 to 47	Chimney pots and slates removed. Fences blown down etc.	Not applicable	Unless ocean racing — and sometimes even then — craft seek deep water. Run towing warps etc. This may be survival force for most	High waves. Dense streaks of foam along the wind. Crests begin to topple, tumble and roll over
10	Storm (Whole gale)	48 to 55	Very rare inland. Trees uprooted; considerable structural damage	Not applicable	Almost the ultimate for yachts. Only chance in deep water and with sea room to run before it or possibly lie to a sea anchor	Very high waves with long overhanging crests. The whole surface of the sea takes on a white appearance. Tumbling of sea heavy and shocklike. Visibility impaired

(taken from *Instant Wind Forecasting*, Peter Davies Ltd 1975)

The time periods within which the wind is expected to rise to the force indicated are described by:

'imminent'   within 6 hours of time of issue
'soon'   between 6 and 12 hours
'later'   more than 12 hours after time of issue

Descriptions of wind strength in land area forecasts

Because the wind is considerably slowed by the land it can be rough at sea when only moderate winds are forecast for land areas. The following table gives the terms used and their equivalents in knots and Beaufort force together with a description of the maximum state of sea which can occur. As winds are slowed over the land more at night than during the day, so the wind speed at sea can be correspondingly higher when a given wind speed is forecast for land areas overnight. The on-shore winds have been assumed to have a 100 mile open sea fetch (180 km).

| Term | Average speed near the ground | Beaufort force | Likely sea conditions 10 miles offshore | | |
			Wind blowing off-shore Day or night	Wind blowing on-shore Day	Night
Calm	less than 1 knot	0	calm	calm or smooth	
Light	1 to 10 knots	1 to 3	smooth to slight	moderate	rough
Moderate	11 to 16 knots	4	smooth to slight	moderate	rough
Fresh	17 to 21 knots	5	moderate	very rough	very rough
Strong	22 to 33 knots	6 to 7	rough	high	very high
Gale	34 to 40 knots	8	rough	survival	
Severe gale	over 40 knots	9 or more	very rough	conditions for yachts	

Note that gale or severe gale conditions are rarely experienced inland, but when the land area forecast says 'fresh to strong' then listen out for the gale warnings at sea.

11 Some April gales

We can learn something useful about gales from taking an actual example of a gale-filled period between 9 and 13 April 1965. These winds were recorded at the exposed Portland Bill lighthouse. The directions were mainly between SW and NW, but speed is our only criterion here so direction is ignored.

At the start of the gales the wind took about seven or eight hours to rise to the middle of Force 6 (about 25 knots) from very light. This is well in accordance with previous research done on the rise times of gales in the English Channel (see *Wind and Sailing Boats*, David and Charles 1973) where it was found that for the sailing months of April to October the

figure 11.1

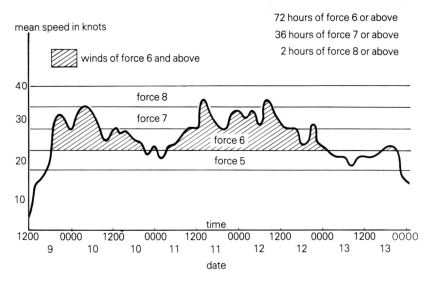

mean speed in knots

72 hours of force 6 or above
36 hours of force 7 or above
2 hours of force 8 or above

An analysis of some April gales in 1965 recorded at Portland Bill, Dorset.

average time for the wind to rise from a manageable 15 knots to a potentially dangerous 25 knots was between seven and eight hours with the shortest time being three hours. So while there is nothing sure in meteorology it can be taken as a rule that when gales are forecast you can stay at sea on a rising wind for at least three hours and often longer. Or, put another way, gales do not suddenly blow up without some warning on the majority of occasions and if you find it getting lumpy you still have a few hours to make a haven before it gets impossible.

Having made this important point let us return to the description of the gales as recorded at Portland (see figure 11.1).

For the following 14 hours, ie right through the night and on into the forenoon of the following day, the wind was Force 7 (verging on 8 once) but no gale warning need have been issued except if the gusts were expected to be repeatedly above 43 knots. With sustained winds around 30 knots and above most cruising yachts would have had to make shelter and the length of the blow meant that the waves would have built to maximum height for the wind speed in question.

For the next 26 hours the wind went down to Force 6 and occasionally to Force 5, but never fell below 20 knots mean speed. Then for an equal period there came the real blow with winds always in Force 7 and twice into Force 8 followed by a slow subsidence that took some 36 hours to complete. Only twice in this period of yacht gales would an official gale warning have been justified and even then the periods of Force 8 were only

51

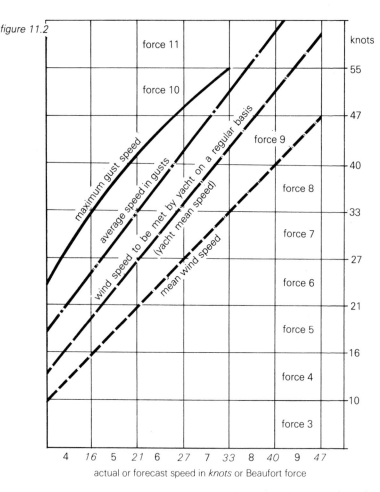

figure 11.2

force 11

force 10

force 9

force 8

force 7

force 6

force 5

force 4

force 3

knots

55

47

40

33

27

21

16

10

maximum gust speed

average speed in gusts

wind speed to be met by yacht on a regular basis
(yacht mean speed)

mean wind speed

| 4 | 16 | 5 | 21 | 6 | 27 | 7 | 33 | 8 | 40 | 9 | 47 |

actual or forecast speed in *knots* or Beaufort force

How to assess the strength of a variable wind. The Yacht Mean Speed, which takes account of gusts, is a better criterion of wind speed for a yacht than the usually quoted Mean Speed.

of about an hour's duration. Yet to the cruising yacht this would have been a dangerously stormy period with long-sustained winds whose gusts would occasionally have been into Force 9. Such conditions would have been unpleasant, but not specifically dangerous, to the merchantman or the frigate – to the yacht they could mean potential disaster.

An often overlooked reason for this lies in the fact that the yacht has to meet the strongest wind that blows, however short its duration. Thus average speeds do not mean much to a yacht struggling to meet even shortlived periods of wind that are far stronger than the mean. By measuring the strength of the gusts that habitually go with certain mean wind speeds we can construct a graph that shows just what the yacht has to meet in the way of wind.

In figure 11.2 select the Beaufort force that you actually expect or is forecast, say Force 6. The first line you come to is the mean speed of the wind (27 knots maximum). The line above that is the average speed in gusts at that Beaufort force (41 knots maximum). The top line is the maximum speed you can expect in gusts and then probably only in association with showers or thunderstorms (in this case 49 knots).

Somewhere in between these speeds is an average speed that the yacht has to meet on a regular basis. It is higher than the mean speed and lower than the average gust speed. We can call it the 'yacht mean speed' and its value is the dashed line in the figure.

You see at once that if Force 6 is in being or forecast the YMS is verging on Force 8 and at Force 7 it is well into 9. This follows because the helmsman has to respond to and meet the sudden gusts and lulls in the wind. It is the strongest wind that heels the yacht on a regular basis that is the criterion and not some rather arbitrary 'mean speed' averaged for some other purposes.

12 What will the waves be like?

When considering a passage you have to listen to the forecast to see what they say about wind shifts that may come along due to the passage of fronts or pressure centres. In this way you are in a better position to assess the likely wave conditions because to do that adequately you need to have an estimate of how long the wind will have blown in a more-or-less constant direction and what its fetch will be.

Fetch is the distance from the nearest land over which the wind can entrain the sea surface and force it into waves. If the wind shifts, the fetch will almost certainly change so that what was a sheltered area is suddenly exposed or vice versa. The further effect of wind shift is to create cross-seas where the waves from say a SW wind ahead of a cold front suddenly meet those pushed on by the NW wind behind the front. The collision of the two wave trains leads to chaotic seas for a time; these may be very difficult to meet and odd eruptions of wave tops can bring sudden deluges of water inboard. Not necessarily dangerous but disconcerting when you are already struggling to meet a new wind direction that perhaps you had not anticipated. For this reason always use any strange wave formation that appears as a prompt to search the environs for a change in

figure 12.1

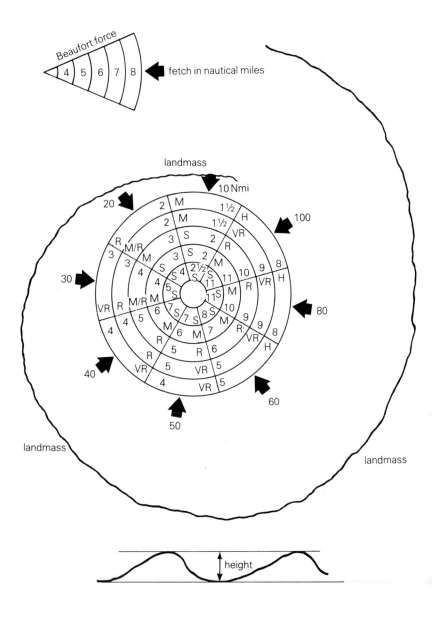

How to assess the likely state of sea when wind force, fetch and duration are known (see table on page 56).

the cloudbase to lighter or darker. The sharper cold fronts reveal almost their exact moment of passing and attendant wind shift by the curious way their lower clouds move in apparently impossible relative directions. This 'churning' of the clouds is the aerial equivalent of the cross-sea mentioned above. One may precede the other and give warning of the shift to come. Assume starboard tack if you can to meet the clockwise shift that goes with the passage of a front – especially a cold front.

Work on a six-hours-ahead principle in assessing the greatest fetch and the maximum wind speed to expect in the coming passage and then use figure 12.1 to predict the most likely wave height you will have to meet. The letters indicate the sea condition to be expected and numbers the time it will take to reach that height. For example, with the wind blowing Force 6 from a mainland shore that is 30 miles away the sea conditions will be moderate to rough and this height will be reached if the wind continues to blow at this speed and in this direction for a full four hours. The height will not increase if the Force 6 'yacht gale' goes on blowing for longer than this. Waves build with time, but there is a limit to their height under a given Beaufort force so once enough time has elapsed (in this case four hours) the waves will not get bigger.

There is also no increase in wave height with distance from a mainland shore (fetch) once a certain fetch has been exceeded. From the figure it is obvious that with Forces 3, 4, 5 and 6 any distance over 50 miles will not add to the wave height. Only with Force 7 or 8, or stronger, will the wave height increase with fetch and then a practical limit is 80 miles.

The waves considered here are those due to the wind that is blowing and in this context we must not forget that swell may exist running under and through the local seaway. Swell is waves made at some other point than where you are and this point may be hundreds of miles away. So the swell is usually quite unrelated to the locally generated seaway. Often, when you push out in the relatively light conditions that may follow a recent storm, the major part of the wave field is swell, and the swell can go on running for a considerable time. On the other hand when swell appears under a slight seaway in gentle or moderate conditions ascertain its direction. It will warn of a severe storm in being way out in the ocean in the direction from which the swell travels. The forecast will tell you if that storm is likely to get to you eventually.

When swell and locally generated seaway (usually of shorter wavelength than the swell) combine, the result will be the occasional addition of a swell crest to a seaway crest so that a larger than normal wave is generated. To allow for this add a foot to the height of the seaway in gale or approaching gale conditions and proportionately less in lighter conditions.

The probability that these effects will create locally enhanced waves increases in storms and when storms continue to blow for many hours in one direction – as happens in the Channel when deep depressions become slow-moving across the north of the country – then the maximum wave height expected must be increased by a third. For example with a 40-mile fetch in the Channel and the wind blowing a sustained Force 7 for some four hours the expected wave height should be 12 ft. The 'storm factor' will warn that now and again 16-ft waves must be expected.

Not only is wave height of importance to the cruising yachtsman, so too is the wavelength of the seaway. If it is too short the result of the slither down the back of the wave that is just passing is to bury the bows in the following wave. The smaller your craft the less this is likely to happen.

When waves run into the shallows their speed decreases but as the same kinetic energy is in the wave field the waves increase in height to compensate. Retardation by the bottom makes them break in a way which, in deep water, is only experienced in storm conditions. This is not really a book concerned with storm conditions. It is expected that the cruising yacht, not being under the same imperative stress as a racing yacht, will seek shelter before the wind rises to anything like storm force. However the prudent skipper should allow for the unthinkable, and read up on heavy weather survival techniques in a book like K. Adlard Coles *Heavy Weather Sailing* (Adlard Coles 1975). State of Sea is a useful, internationally understood, code to describe the size of the larger well-formed waves in the surrounding wave field.

Code figure	Descriptive terms	Wave height		French terms
		feet	metres	
0	calm (glassy)	0	0	calme
1	calm (rippled)	0 to 4 in	0 to 0.1	calme (ridée)
2	smooth (wavelets)	4 in to 20 in	0.1 to 0.5	belle
3	slight	20 in to 4 ft	0.5 to 1.25	peu agitée
4	moderate	4 ft to 8 ft	1.25 to 2.5	agitée
5	rough	8 ft to 13 ft	2.5 to 4	forte
6	very rough	13 ft to 20 ft	4 to 6	très forte
7	high	20 ft to 30 ft	6 to 9	grosse
8	very high	30 ft to 45 ft	9 to 14	très grosse
9	phenomenal	Over 45 ft	Over 14	énorme

13 Visibility

The meteorological elements that obscure visibility are relatively few. Rain, unless it is heavy, will not of itself greatly reduce visibility but drizzle will. Snow will cut visibility rapidly to a few yards, especially when the flurries are from spring-time shower clouds – the major time when cruising and snow are likely to meet. Otherwise fog or mist produces most loss of visibility at sea, but even in these cases there are some situations more prone to poor visibility than others. If the foggy air has come from some source which is industrial the visibility will be cut dramatically in fog that otherwise would only be verging on mistiness. This happens with some easterly winds in the North Sea and Channel when the wind has blown from the industrial areas of Belgium, Northern France and Holland. Visibility often falls on the east coast of England for this reason and if the air is already close to becoming foggy the smoke particles accelerate the action. Such fogs are mixtures of water drops and smoke particles and that is, or used to be, the recipe for smogs in London and other industrial cities. Clean air acts have made for fewer manmade fogs and so fewer coastwise fogs when the wind is blowing off-shore.

As the prevailing winds are westerly we might expect the East to be more fog-prone than the West and in a way that is true of fogs that are industrially enhanced. However the worst of the sea fogs, which are pure water-drop fogs, are to be found on the wings of the SW wind when warm, moist air is dragged up from the subtropical seas by the right sets of isobars. Whenever the isobars stream, unbroken, back down towards the Azores, or the sea wastes between there and America, you must expect extensive fog around the coasts that face south and west.

It cannot be categorically stated that there is any wind direction that can be considered free from fog. Fog can turn up on any coast at some time or other, but certain stretches are more fog prone than others. One notorious one in summer is the Helgoland Bight and a secondary one is Dover Strait. Quite a large incidence of fog is found off Western Scotland in summer and, south of Iceland, the frequency increases to an average of over five hours in a period of four days.

Coastwise cruising in the early morning leaves you prone to radiation fog that has drifted off the land during the night and such fog may persist off the coast (if it has been carried that far) while the land fog has long since been 'burned-off' by the sun. This follows because the major factor that clears fog ashore is the heating of the ground under the fog bank. Often this layer in the morning is not very deep and from high ground valleys; the tops of steeples and high buildings generally sticking incongruously out of the top of the fog layer are common sights. In late spring and summer morning fog ashore is almost certain to go because the layer allows heat to penetrate it. Of itself it does not absorb the sun's rays, but it will absorb the longer heat rays from the ground and so set up convection currents and clear – sometimes like magic. No such help is to be gained from the sea which is not heated by the sun and if the coastal fogginess of the morning is to go it must be by 'advection' (ie transport sideways as opposed to convention which is transport in the vertical). One 'advector' of the morning fog banks is sea breezes following in the wake of the clearance of the fog ashore (see page 78). Also wind tends to get up during the morning which may blow the fog somewhere else and occasionally disperse it all together.

Visibility may well be below fog limits near the centres of lows and especially when the shipping forecast goes for 'winds, cyclonic variable'. In such conditions cloudbase may be not far off the sea surface and drizzle or fine rain be dense and persistent. The only real help with 'when will it clear?' is to be gained from the shift in the wind. If the wind sticks to one direction then usually the conditions will stick as well. What you are looking for is a change in the cloudbase, perhaps a lighter patch coming along. Then the conditions can change, often for the better. If it suddenly gets much clearer suspect that a cold front is passing or at least in the offing.

Fogginess ashore is not associated with strong winds except over high ground, but over the sea it may be blowing Force 7 to 8 and be very murky indeed so that lights are not visible until you are on top of them. Such conditions test the navigator to the utmost. However they are nearly always associated with fronts or depression centres and therefore need not last overlong.

Fog, mist and visibility limits

Visibility is of immense importance to the yachtsman because he is relatively close to the sea. So his horizon is that much nearer, and visibility that is closing in may not be noticeable until the horizon is lost. The sea horizon is a mere 3.63 Nmi miles away when the eye is 10 ft above the sea (5.8 km at 3 m).

By international agreement these are the limits for mist and fog:

Mist   visibility between 1 and 2 km (1100–2200 yds)
Fog   visibility less than 1 km (1100 yds)

However these limits are for aviation and for other purposes lower limits must be fixed and defined.

Description of visibility in land area forecasts
Dense fog less than 55 yds (50 m)
Fog   less than 220 yds (200 m)
Mist   less than 1100 yds (1 km)

Description of visibility in sea area forecasts
Fog   less than 1100 yds (1 km)
Poor   less than 2 nautical miles (3½ km)
Moderate less than 5 nautical miles (9 km)
Good   over 5 nautical miles (9 km)

Description of visibility in coastal station actual reports and aviation forecasts

| Fog | less than 1100 yds (1 km) |
| Mist or haze | less than 2200 yds (2 km) |

14 Terms used in forecasts

Because certain weather conditions produce definitely different sky conditions, the phrases chosen by forecasters can mean more than would appear at first sight.

For daylight periods

	Meaning	Inferences
Bright	Considerable diffuse sunshine and perhaps some direct sunshine as well	The sky is covered with a veil of thin high cloud. Often associated with coming or stationary fronts and with coming thundery conditions
Bright periods	Bright sky for more than half the time	There are often two cloud layers – a bright high one and a darker lower one with large holes in it
Bright intervals	Intermittent occurrences of a bright sky between more prevalent dark sky	This can be associated with old fronts such as occlusions and cover wide areas
Cloudy	Cloud is extensive and thick enough to look dark	The cloudy conditions can be due to low cloud or cloud of the medium levels
Dry	No precipitation or thick fog	It may be cloudy and dry
Dull	Complete cover of cloud which is so thick as to need a stronger term than cloudy	This is the sky associated with cyclonic conditions, with active fronts or wet sea winds
Fine	As Dry but some sunshine as well	Associated with anticyclonic conditions

For daylight periods

	Meaning	*Inferences*
Sunny	Sunshine most of the time	The weather associated with ridges of high pressure and anticyclonic conditions
Sunny periods	Fairly continuous sunshine for an hour or two at a time, and more sunshine than cloud	Often fair days with cumulus clouds. The airstream is frequently returning maritime Polar air
Sunny intervals	Intermittent sunshine with more cloud than sun	Wetter airstreams which build cumulus clouds or where these clouds spread under temperature inversions

Showers

Showers	More-or-less continuous processions of showers expected throughout the period	Airstream definitely colder than the sea or land. Recently out of a maritime Polar source region. There may be heavy gusts in the showers. Expect it to be cold and damp for the time of year. Chances of a clap of thunder and some hail. Unexpected snow may occur at either end of the season, with loss of visibility
Occasional showers	Only a few showers expected during the period. Long clear periods between	Airstream cooler than the land or sea, but not greatly so. Also not as damp as with Showers. Airstream has spent some time away from its Polar source region. Can be warm and pleasant between showers
Thundery showers	Rain may be in heavy downpours accompanied by thunder and lightning	Rather rare over oceans. In confined waters like the North Sea or English Channel, associated with thundery conditions over the adjacent land

Showers

	Meaning	*Inferences*
Showers perhaps thunder	Showers which may be heavy (possibly with hail) can grow big enough to become thunderstorms	Probably the showers will be isolated, but will be severe when they do occur. Now and again a bigger than usual shower will produce thunder and lightning. There may be some rather heavy gusts when the showers and/or storms strike

Fog

Fog patches	When fog is likely to occur but not continuous in time or position	Airstream is just a little warmer than the sea temperature (which may be estimated), so probably rather cloudy, but otherwise fair. Wind cannot be very strong. Airmass originally from a Tropical maritime quarter
Fog	When fog is very likely to occur and be widespread	Airstream definitely warmer than the sea temperature and also humid. Very wet air or drizzle also likely to occur. It can be totally overcast and if sufficient wind there may be a very low amorphous layer of stratus. Again wind speed not great. Airstream usually directly from a Tropical maritime quarter
Coastal fog patches	Visibility at sea is expected to be better than along the coast	Above remarks (Fog patches) generally apply. Can be associated with thundery conditions in which case thunderstorms can approach without being seen. Rare for fog to survive the passage of the thunder

Rain

	Meaning	*Inferences*
Rain	Continuous rain is expected during the period	A slow-moving frontal, trough system or depression centre will remain in the area during the period. However if rain is expected throughout the period, even with some brief respites, this term will be used
Rain at times	Rain will occur, go on for a period and then die out to recur later	Rain of this nature usually comes from fairly high nimbostratus clouds and visibility is usually good. The airstream is often one ahead of a warm front or occlusion or it may be the warm sector of a depression
Occasional rain	Rainy periods are relatively short	Between the rainy patches the sky remains overcast unlike showers where the sky clears. Again old fronts or troughs are often responsible for this kind of desultory rainfall. Visibility is usually good
Intermittent rain	Rainy periods are relatively long	The sky again remains overcast, but it will be wetter than when the rain is described as Occasional. Visibility may not be as good in this case
Thundery rain	Heavy rain at times but variable in intensity. It can be both occasional or intermittent and there may be thunder	This is the rain from an unstable warm front or occlusion and it can be very wet indeed. High level storms may sear the sea with bolts of lightning. Visibility may be poor

Rain

	Meaning	*Inferences*
Outbreaks of rain	Can cover Occasional, Intermittent and Rain at times when over a long period of a forecast different forms will occur	A useful term for the forecaster who does not quite know how the rain will occur or who cannot otherwise describe it adequately
Rain spreading	The term used when a front or trough is going to produce rain later	Almost always the basis of the term is the appearance on the weather map of a warm front or occlusion moving into the area in the forecast period. Note if the term 'cyclonic' is used with the wind forecast because then the rain will be due to being close to a depression centre and can be prolonged with extensive overcast and possibly poor visibility
Showers at first rain later	In cyclonic weather an unstable airstream will stabilize, there will be a short respite before warm frontal weather begins to encroach	An unstable airstream in a trough behind one depression centre just passed is probably going to be replaced by another warm front of a following depression. The wind forecast ought to be for backing and increasing wind. Visibility usually remains good to excellent, even exceptional

Thunderstorms

Widespread and heavy	Storms will be of the most intense kind. There will be reports of damage and occasional loss of life from being struck. These usually occur inland but on occasions prodigious storms move over the sea	These are heat storms set off in sultry unstable air usually confined to summer but also occasionally in spring and autumn. These storms will usually 'clear the air' ie tomorrow's weather will be cooler and probably fair

Thunderstorms

	Meaning	Inferences
Scattered	Such storms may be locally heavy and may result in cloudbursts over land. With a long sea track they are mixed with non-thundery but heavy showers. They can occur at any time of the year	The airstream is often quite cool. Very different from the overheated feel that goes with the widespread storms of summer. The airstream is a more than usually humid one and often indicates a virgin form of the Polar maritime airstream, especially in spring
Frontal	Storms will come mixed up with more continuous rain from a front. The base of such storm cells is often as much as 8000 ft (2½ km) up and so most lightning is from cloud to cloud with reverberating thunder and only occasional flashes to the ground	The forecast will not usually describe storms that occur on fronts as frontal but the general synopsis may indicate that storms to follow are going to break out on a coming front. Storms set off this way may go on for a long time. They are the ones that produce 'summer lightning' over the sea

15 Terms used to describe pressure systems

Term	Meaning	Remarks
Trough of low pressure	A more-or-less deep cyclonic kink in the isobars without an obvious front in it. Expect showers and squalls in the trough – sometimes thunderstorms. Not usually of long duration	Troughs stick out round low centre like spokes of a wheel. The frontal ones contain warm and cold fronts or occlusions. The frontal trough has different airmass characteristics either side of it. The trough is usually in the cold air and the airmasses are the same either side. When drawing

Term	Meaning	Remarks
		troughs kink your isobars cyclonically and write 'Trough' along the axis
Weak trough	Cyclonic rather than anticyclonic weather here. Winds only moderate or light	The weak trough is only a shallow cyclonic kink in the isobars. You could even ignore it and write 'Weak Trough' in the region it is supposed to occupy
Low 998	Here is a depression centre you can plot on a forecast chart. Its central pressure is 998 millibars (see page 91 for conversion to inches)	Most shipping or coastal forecasts will give pressure centres and their expected movements and central pressures now and at the end of the forecast period. Knowledge of the structure of depressions helps add a wealth of detail to such a simple statement
Deep low	Term used to emphasize that the centre is encased in many rings of isobars and therefore winds will be gale or severe gale somewhere in its compass	Deep lows are also 'intense' lows and, in general, weather conditions will be at their worst. The worst weather is often not near the centre, but further away. Frontal systems tend to be sharper and their features correspondingly intense. Unexpected deteriorations occur without much regard for the accepted theory of depressions. Squalls are an ever-present threat
Shallow low	Term emphasizes that only a few isobaric rings will enclose this centre on the analyzed chart from which the forecast was made up	Winds will be light, but weather cloudy, probably poor visibility or even fog. In summer shallow lows can lose their cloud and become the seats of intense thunderstorms (overland, but not over the sea)

65

Term	Meaning	Remarks
Associated frontal trough or troughs	Means that you can try drawing the fronts back into the low centre	Many fronts are divisions between very modified and old airmasses that have lost all contact with the low with which they formed. This term emphasizes younger frontal systems
Cyclonic	The winds will shift in a manner that accompanies the close passage of a low centre. The term is used in this sense in forecasts but in another sense meteorologically (see page 147). It appears when it would be impossible to describe the wind shifts involved	For example the passage of a low to the south of the observer will yield easterly winds followed by northerly and then by winds with westerly components, ie the wind continually backs. If the low passes to the north the wind may be SE to start with, but continually veers. If the centre passes over the observer there will be light variable winds or even calm before the wind picks up from a point that has westerly components

(The term 'anticyclonic' is not used in the same sense as above because no highs traverse an area to produce wind shifts that cannot adequately be described in the forecast.)

Term	Meaning	Remarks
Deepening	This indicates a developing depression so you can expect an intensification of the whole complex	The emphasis is on the young depression that still has not reached maturity. So there may be several days of life in it yet. It can be expected to bring features ahead of it pretty certainly into its circulation so that cols over an area will disappear and weak ridges (or even strong ridges) will be devoured
Vigorous	Strong winds and often intense rainfall. Such lows may also travel fast and deepen as they go.	Often young Polar-front depressions or secondaries gain this description. The low may not be large (large

Term	Meaning	Remarks
	Cyclonic weather at its worst	lows like large people tend not to be vigorous), but sketching it on a chart means surrounding its centre with lots of isobars. Note if it is also deepening. If it is, and is headed for you as well, seek shelter NOW.
Complex	At least two main centres plus perhaps a few lesser satellite centres	The chart feature that looks like 'two fried eggs' is a complex low. Treat it like a dumb-bell. It will rotate about its combined centre of gravity. If one low is bigger than the other the smaller one tends to gyrate round the larger. Such systems are loth to move and bring nasty, but not usually dangerous, cyclonic weather to the area for days on end
Filling	A depression past its prime with the barometer generally rising. Often slow moving in the later stages. Winds moderate but visibility may deteriorate	Occluding depressions fill. So this term with 'associated frontal trough' or troughs means that the latter is partly an occlusion. It will become more of an occlusion as time progresses
Blocking anticyclone or high	Continuation of present weather pattern for days and possibly weeks	Blocking highs bring anticyclonic weather to the areas they dominate, but induce unseasonal weather to peripheral areas. Thus if a blocking high dominates Atlantic Europe, Spain may experience a run of unfamiliar lows
Anticyclone or high (travelling)	Anticyclonic wind-shift pattern will traverse the areas along the path of the anticyclone	Time scale here for continuation of anticyclonic weather is a day or two with considerable variation in the

Term	Meaning	Remarks
		weather and wind patterns in any area as the high moves past
Anticyclone or high (stationary or quasi-stationary)	Situation will remain static with some minor variations. However the encroachment of depressions will tighten the gradient and wind can get strong	An apparently set-fair forecast but considerable deterioration in wind and sea conditions can occur when a high will not move in the face of pressure from impinging lows. On the edges of highs sustained winds of long fetch can produce very big seas
Ridge of high pressure (travelling)	Between lows this is perhaps the only chance you will have to slip from one haven to another	Winds lighten into the ridge behind a retreating low and then back before the next low. Otherwise the ridge may be a change in the way the isobars curve in an otherwise fairly static situation. The barometer in any case will be on the rise at first, before it tips over later
Ridge of high pressure (stationary or quasistationary)	This is just an outrider from a Blocking or Stationary anticyclone, so remarks there apply	

16 Speed of movement of pressure systems

When the forecast says that a depression is moving rather quickly northeast the term 'rather quickly' is not arbitrary. The following are the speeds that go with the descriptions:

Slowly	up to 15 knots
Steadily	15 to 25 knots

Rather quickly	25 to 35 knots
Rapidly	35 to 45 knots
Very rapidly	over 45 knots

In general depressions obey the following rules:

i a depression that moves rapidly does not deepen

ii depressions that move very rapidly must be small and are often only waves on a cold front trailing from some much larger depression

iii a depression that moves steadily or rather quickly and deepens at the same time will be a strong disturbance

iv depressions that move slowly may be moderate sized systems that are deepening or they may be old filling depressions

v the term quasi-stationary is also used to indicate systems that are almost rooted to one spot. Complex low pressure systems are often quasi-stationary

vi if the forecast says that a depression is moving fast and at the same time it goes for it deepening expect winds of gale or strong gale force

Travelling anticyclones will also have speeds of movement described by these terms, but it will be very rare for the terms 'rapidly' or 'very rapidly' to be used concerning travelling highs.

Highs are more likely to be quasi-stationary and if it appears that an anticyclone is more-or-less immobile over a certain region and a low is described as moving towards it at any speed expect strong or even gale force winds to occur between the two systems. This is particularly likely when a blocking anticyclone has been over a region for many days or weeks and Atlantic lows are trying to break it down. It is often loth to leave – and the longer it has been there the more sluggish it is likely to be so that the breakdown to cyclonic weather may take days to achieve. During much of this time southerly gales can blow on the flank of the anticyclone only made more acceptable because the white horses drive by under fair skies.

17 Sailing weather zones

When cruising you frequent three different regions of the coastal weather scene. You are always going to spend a good deal of time in the landlocked waters of harbours, creeks, estuaries and étangs. In fact when starting cruising it is a good plan to sail small waters and perhaps never poke your nose into the open sea. In this way you get to know the boat and your own capabilities. You have to learn all those things you will need to know on putting into an unknown haven – the way the tides act, how to keep off the mud (which will entail a good deal of actual boat handling) and become used to the ways and wiles of harbourmasters.

When you sail such waters the weather you have is almost entirely land weather. You will get little or no help from shipping forecasts here and inshore waters' forecasts need modifying. Unless there is a direct blow from the open sea the wind will be less strong than forecast for the open sea, especially at low water when the shelter of the shores has increased to a maximum. The wind variations will be greatest in these landlocked waters and the full effect of the daily (diurnal) variation in the wind speed, cloudiness, temperature and humidity will be felt.

The major dangers you face in restricted waters like these include being caught on an ebb when it is running at full belt out of a harbour against a wind blowing up strongly into the entrance. Also the difficulties of finding your way safely amongst a crowd of craft that are either moored or sailing, when you have less sea room than you would like. On the other hand the close proximity of the shore makes it feel more secure – although often the sheer fact of the confined space in which you have to manoeuvre means the opposite.

Once you seek the open sea you are in the coastwise weather zone. Here the weather is greatly influenced by the land when the wind comes from any point landward, but it is also an 'offshore' zone when the wind blows unhampered from seaward. In coastal cruising you will often go from potentially landlocked situations between islands, or an island and the mainland, into a coastal zone where the wind has more fetch and then into an offshore situation as your position, with respect to the land, changes.

A coastal zone is rather like landlocked waters with waves when the wind blows off-shore; rather like offshore waters but with greater risks when the wind blows on-shore and is also the zone where seabreezes start and hold sway on light-weather days. After dark it is the zone where the nocturnal winds blow in light weather, but it can also be the place where the wind gathers to its strongest when the big blow comes along.

The third zone is the offshore one and here I assume you are beyond the reach of the land – although in the English Channel for example, or the southern North Sea it is rare for anyone making passage from one side to another not to have weather and wind influenced by the land masses. On the other hand if you cruise down the Atlantic coast of France your chances of being in almost pure offshore weather are very high because the coast is exposed to the prevailing wind directions. Because of its situation the Atlantic coast of North America is more likely to experience coastwise weather.

The attributes of the offshore zone are mainly negative ones. There will be no diurnal variation in wind speed as we expect; very little change in air temperature except when airmasses change; seabreeze and landbreeze effects will be far less than further inshore. Cloudiness at low level will

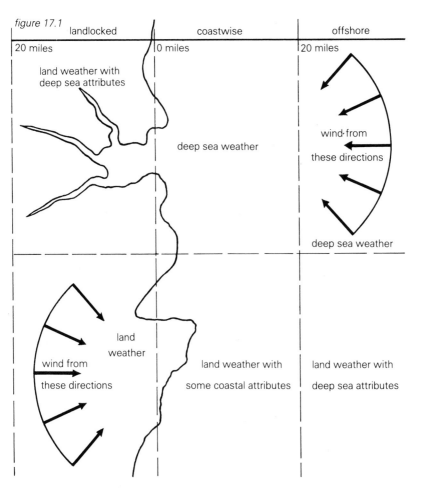

figure 17.1

| landlocked | coastwise | offshore |

20 miles

land weather with
deep sea attributes

0 miles

deep sea weather

20 miles

wind from

these directions

deep sea weather

wind from

these directions

land
weather

land weather with

some coastal attributes

land weather with

deep sea attributes

*Attributes of the sailing weather zones. When winds are more parallel to
the coast the conditions are likely to be somewhere between the ones given.*

usually be the result of the sea temperature being higher than the air
temperature and the cloud will often not assume the neat crisp globular
shapes experienced ashore, but be ragged and ill formed. Higher cloud is
almost certainly something to do with fronts, either fronts forming or
fronts dying or, more normally, fronts just existing. The weather of the
offshore zone is more purely oceanic in character so that fronts are often
more clearly defined and their effects more marked. However between
fronts the weather is mainly under the influence of the relative temperatures of airstreams and sea surface to which we have to add the attributes
of the airmass above our heads to either help or hinder convection
currents. It is a fact that on the whole the cloud of the oceans is cumulus

because statistically the sea surface temperature tends to be a degree or so greater than that of the overlying air.

The attributes of the weather zones can be tied up in a diagram (see figure 17.1).

18 Wind near the coast

When the wind blows from the land to the sea its speed is going to be up to two Beaufort forces more when it leaves the shelter of the land. This must always be borne in mind when setting out, especially at night.

The calming effect over the land at night is very great after days when the wind has been up to Force 4 during the day, and is still noticeable even with stronger winds. When winds blow parallel to the coastline there will often be an even more marked contrast between the wind in landlocked surroundings and when breaking clear of the harbour bar. This is particularly noticeable on the south coast of England if the general wind direction is easterly.

When you are contemplating leaving harbour for the open sea you will want to know the wind speed and direction, and on many occasions this information will be sought from land stations. On the other hand you may have a masthead anemometer or be in touch with someone who has, or your club may have one which you can consult. In this event you have a more-or-less reliable actual reading of the wind speed.

In some ways that is as useful as a forecast, except when the situation is very changeable, because you can make your own estimate of the wind strength at sea.

Winds from a direction with at least 5–10 miles fetch over land

Beaufort force at shore station	Wind speed in knots	Likely wind strength at sea	
		By day	By night
0–1	0–3	1–3	1–4
2	4–6	4	4–5
3	7–10	4–5	5
4	11–16	5	5–6
5	17–21	6–7	7
6	22–27	7–8	8
7	28–33	8–9	9–10

It will be seen that the wind speed to expect by night is usually one Beaufort force up on the value you would expect by day and in its turn the daytime wind at sea is likely to be two Beaufort forces up on light winds recorded ashore, but one force up when the winds strengthen.

When winds blow from seaward the effect of the land is less marked, but observations made by the author at Hurn Airport some 4 miles inland from the coastline of Poole Bay compared with winds at Portland Bill lighthouse, which is almost wholly exposed to the on-shore winds, show that such a relatively short fetch over the land can have a very marked effect on the wind. Thus anyone who rings up a 'coastal' airfield or similar for their wind strength must allow for the increases given below to assess the wind at sea:

Winds from a direction on-shore and with a few miles land fetch

Beaufort force at shore station	Wind speed in knots	Likely wind strength at sea	
		By day	By night
0–3	0–10	1–4	1–5
4	11–16	4–5	5–6
5	17–21	6	7
6	22–27	7–8	8–9
7	28–33	8–9	9–10

The trends outlined in Coastal Winds (see pages 183–6) through the 24 hours should be considered as there may be explanations of effects for which there is no obvious reason. One such is the way that easterly winds in the English Channel by night may be almost calm over the land and yet be blowing Force 4–5 at sea. As usual the night winds tend to be most different between land and sea but with easterlies the daytime winds at sea are often twice as strong as they are ashore. Easterlies in the Channel however rarely exceed Force 6.

It is useful to mention here that with winds that blow parallel to a coastline by day and continue to do so into the evening and night there will be a speed-up over the sea to compensate for the slowing down of the wind over the land with the onset of evening. Conversely in the morning as the wind over the land picks up in speed the wind over the sea will often go lighter to compensate.

In the above tables the effects of sea breezes and nocturnal winds on the lighter winds that blow must be considered, but in either case the skies need to be relatively clear of cloud for the gradient winds to be taken over by the local effects.

The coastal wind has a definite tendency to blow on-shore by day and off-shore by night; this is very well illustrated by the wind statistics from any reliable coastal weather station. For example at Southport in Lancashire which looks out into Liverpool Bay the number of winds from seaward doubles between dawn and 1400 while the winds from landward reach maximum frequency around dawn and are three times less frequent by the afternoon (see figure 53.3).

When sizeable mountains exist not far inland the effect may be very marked indeed and a case in point is Biarritz at the southern end of the Atlantic coast of France which at 0600 in spring, for example, has two chances in every three of having winds from the general direction of the Pyrenees. By 1800 winds from these directions have become the least frequent and now there is the same high chance of having winds from seaward.

Thus the coastwise region is the most likely one to have winds that shift and the likely periods for change are when the on-shore seabreezes are being established between 0800 and 1200 by the sun, and the corresponding evening period when the overnight wind is picking up from landward between 2000 and midnight.

19 When showers are forecast

The term 'showers' can mean many different things. In sea areas the showers are formed when the air is cooler than the sea surface, but they may look rather different from the ones we are used to on land. <u>Sea showers are often hidden behind masses of surrounding ragged cloud that has not formed into anything like a cumulus cloud.</u> This is especially so when the airstream is straight out of an ocean and therefore is as wet as it can be.

On the western seaboard NW winds are often very showery as cold air comes south over gradually increasing sea temperatures and so the potential to build shower clouds increases. These showers will not vary greatly by day or night, coming along singly or in groups and with a wide variation in the heaviness of the rain that falls. However expect them to reach maximum frequency in the early hours of the morning; this is exactly opposite to the variation experienced over the land.

Land area forecasts will, just like their vague maritime counterpart, say 'showers' and not qualify the statement by saying when the showers will occur. This is quite understandable because showers are notorious for occurring in some places more than others and for not occurring anywhere when they were expected to do so quite widely. You can take it that away from windward coasts showers are more likely to break out later in the day the further you go from the windward coastline. So on the east coast of

Britain the most likely time for showers, when the wind is from the showery quarter of NW, is lunchtime or just after. When they do come along they may well be part of an 'airmass trough' which looks rather like a cold front as it bears down spewing out cirrus 'anvils' above a mass of bulging cumulonimbus clouds. However it usually passes in an hour and then, because the air has temporarily had its fill of making showers, there is a clear period before a few more isolated showers come along. In the long days of late spring there can be two troughs and the evening one can conceivably become thundery. However such things are rare.

So on windward coasts expect that when the forecast goes for 'showers, some of them heavy', you could get showers at any time of the day or night – and maybe more at night than by day especially when the wind driving them along is not all that strong. This regime will exist and possibly be intensified as the showery air arrives over land warmed by the sun. Deluges of rain will cascade on to the watersheds of mountain and hill ranges and in their lee shower potential becomes less, so that in Eastern Britain (or anywhere to leeward of a ridge) it has to be a fairly wet and unstable airstream that produces intense and frequent showers. It is far more likely that the showers will occur in batches well spaced in time and then along organized trough lines stretched across the wind.

The danger to the cruising yacht from showers comes from the gusts that appear just ahead of them. Expect any shower to as much as double or even treble the wind speed ahead of it and treat them with respect accordingly. The strong wind comes with the falling rain in a squall and then becomes lighter as the shower passes. Only showers of snow or hail greatly impair visibility, and while on the subject remember that the forecast of showers also means good or excellent visibility with no risk of fog. Only thundery showers are likely to be accompanied by poor visibility that may make landfalls difficult or present a hazard in other ways. (We have been talking here of the kind of showers which are built by convection currents from heated land or water, but they are not the only kind of showers and the descriptions of other kinds on page 60 should be studied.)

There are inferences of great importance to be read into the fact that showers, when forecast with a fair degree of confidence, sometimes do not materialize. Perhaps the most important is that the air is stabilizing when it ought to be continuing to be unstable. The stabilizing influence is usually sinking air at altitude coming down like the lid of a pressure cooker to prevent the showers 'boiling up' below. Such an effect is often the herald of another depression on its way sooner than was expected. You should always suspect the sky that ought to be full of shower clouds, but becomes partially covered with layer clouds – often lumpy layers. However, remember that showers over land grow with the day and die with the evening so do not be fooled, by showers that die out at the end of the day, into suspecting that tomorrow will not again be showery. It probably will be and the outlook should confirm it.

When you recognize that the last cold front of a sequence of depressions has passed, the wind usually goes to somewhere around NW. Then showers grow big and frequent and this is the sequence of events that eventually leads to a substantial period of good weather. Firstly a period of big, often anvil-headed shower clouds comes along. These go on for as much as a day or two but gradually transform into a much more benign sky of smaller cumulus clouds. If the better weather comes slowly it will last longer and go slowly as well. It is the short, sharp burst of showers followed by a rapid dying out and clearance that heralds new trouble on the way. Not every time mind you – but most of the time.

One last point of importance. Cold fronts are notorious for growing wave depressions on them. These are often not large, nor vicious, but they can throw veils of cirrus across a recently showery sky. The cold front itself will have passed earlier, perhaps a few hours earlier and the wave will lift it back towards you just like flicking a hump into a rope tied to a stanchion. Often the cumulus clouds below the higher cirrus are shaded and appear dark and forbidding. Certainly a wave is a feature that makes showers die out, but which need not result in any really bad weather. Waves normally run quickly through your area with an increase in cloud, a return of rain that you thought had gone, but not much wind. In summer they may be very thundery, but normally the thunder is set off over the land and not over the sea.

Thus the forecast of 'showers' can mean many things and only experience can sort out the various possibilities. Certainly the forecast of showers which do not strike you, but may be occurring in numbers elsewhere, is one of the major reasons for the public's mistrust of weather forecasts. Bear with the forecasters – to predict where and when showers will occur is impossible. Sometimes there are so many showers that everyone gets some. At other times large areas escape entirely. Coastal waters in the lee of high ground are subject to showers and the falling winds that accompany them. These may be very dangerous as they are akin to the similar down-draught gales that occur on some European lakes. Unlike the latter however the craft at sea has no warning siren like the ones installed on many lakes. Falling winds reach their maximum of severity when they accompany thunderstorms that come from over high ground that looks straight down to the sea.

20 When fog is forecast

Sea fog is most prevalent in late spring and early summer when warmer air masses arrive over seas that are still cold from the winter. It is associated with maritime Tropical airmasses and with wind directions from southern oceans. Slight wind is conducive to its formation, as is a sea fetch of 100 miles or more.

Sometimes coastal fog patches form more readily than fog at sea because of areas of low surface water temperature brought out on the ebb when the tide has flooded during the early hours.

In shipping forecasts the following terms are used:

'Extensive or widespread fog' – this occurs when the dewpoint of the air is everywhere higher than the sea surface temperature.

'Fog banks' – these form when the dewpoint temperature is close to the sea surface temperature. However variable sea temperature does not allow of there being a totally extensive or widespread cover of fog.

'Fog patches' – the dewpoint temperature of the air is only likely to be higher than the sea temperature in a few areas. Fog patches are thinner, less extensive and fewer than fog banks. Coastal fog patches are mainly a phenomenon of winter and spring.

Because of great difficulty in knowing the sea surface temperature forecasters will sometimes forecast sea fog when none will occur. They work on the assumption that the mariner would rather be warned of the possibility of sea fog which does not materialize rather than suddenly be enveloped in it without warning. Sea surface temperature is reported by ships on the main shipping lanes, but is not regularly reported when ships enter home waters. Thus any yachtmaster with a reliable coastal sea surface temperature to report should contact a main forecasting office giving the position and the method by which he obtained the reading. As an ex-forecaster I know how valuable such reports can be when conditions are hovering between 'will it fog' or 'won't it'. Fog over land is due to radiation on clear nights and tends to be a phenomenon of the early morning in summer, but extends its risk period forward into the morning and backwards into the hours before midnight as the winter season approaches. It will sink off coasts and shores on to local waters, but often clears into low stratus along coasts, before dispersing with the day.

On fine sunny mornings in spring and early summer sea fog laying off the coast may be brought in by seabreeze activity so that creeks, harbours and estuaries suddenly become fogbound where only a few minutes before it had been warm and pleasant.

A means of monitoring the position of sea fog is via the actuals from coastal stations broadcast with shipping forecasts. However it must be remembered that when fog banks or patches are forecast the fact that a coastal station is clear of fog is no guarantee that there are not extensive fog areas lurking elsewhere in the area.

Fog can be seen as a low 'cloud bank' on the horizon, but it is often very difficult to assess how far away it is. The loss of sea marks at known distances will give more reliable information on position and possibly, if two such marks exist at different distances, an assessment of how long the bank may take to reach you.

21 About fog

Fog may occur when the airstream is warmer than the sea (or land) over which it travels. It cannot occur when the reverse is the case ie the air is cooler than the surface below it.

This follows from a general principle useful in many situations that *Heat seeks cold* (see section 52). Following this principle indicates that the airstreams with fog potential are ones that are tending to sink on to the surface, but that warmth at the bottom of a cooler airstream will create the convection currents that are death to any foggy air (see figure 21.1).

It follows that the airstreams that are likely to be foggy are ones from the southern quadrants that have come from source regions over the sea. In Britain and Atlantic Europe generally the most likely wind direction for fog is SW. Thus when the forecast goes for fog as well as a SW wind (or a direction surrounding SW) the chance of the forecast being right is very high. That does not preclude foggy airstreams from other directions. For example the Channel is sometimes foggy with E winds especially before summer thunderstorms break out.

When a front becomes more-or-less parallel to the isobars and so moves very slowly there is considerable risk of sudden fogs.

figure 21.1

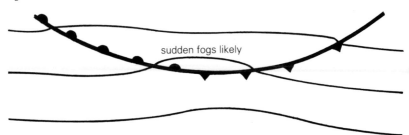

sudden fogs likely

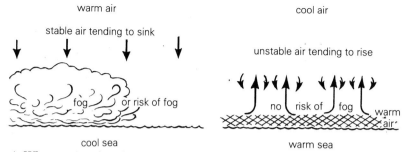

figure 21.2a   *figure 21.2b*

a) *When warm air exists over a cooler sea surface there is fog risk.*
b) *With a sea surface warmer than the air there is no fog risk.*

The latter is worth noting because you might say that it goes entirely contrary to the *Heat seeks cold* principle above. Surely, it will be argued, thunderstorms are the biggest convection currents of all and they go with rising, unstable air. So how can it be foggy? The answer is that the thunderstorms occur along the line of a front, but ahead of the front the air is warm, moist and stable – just the combination for fog.

Often temporary foggy conditions will occur at sea in association with the passage of fronts and depressions. On the weather map suspect the sea areas where a trailing cold front loops back to become the warm front of a following depression (see figure 21.1). The weather will not amount to much in such regions, but often the wind is quite light and the front is in a sort of limbo between its life as a cold front and a new existence as a warm front. Such a 'quasi-stationary' front can be a breeding ground for sudden clamps of dense fog. The fog will often not last many hours, but that is no consolation when caught in waters made dangerous by shipping, shallows, rocks and wrecks. The way the clear conditions just behind a cold front can suddenly and catastrophically become 'soup' conditions, as the front begins to swing back over you as a creeping warm front, have to be experienced to be believed. They are also conditions that may not be suspected and allowed for in the forecast.

The different phrases used to describe fog and its incidence (on page 61) should be studied. Their very sparseness should indicate that little precision in time or place can be expected when fog is forecast for sea areas. In coastwise zones fog formed in coastal valleys during the early night may be wafted over the local waters by the drift of nocturnal winds as they spring up in the hours around midnight. Usually however air cooled over the land at night and which finds its way over the sea will become convective and so keep the night watches clear of fog risk. In this context fog patches that may have lingered near the coast in the warmth of the day can be cleared as night winds begin to blow coolly from landward.

On the other hand the daytime seabreeze can suddenly clamp the coastwise strip and any landlocked waters within its fetch in sea fog; this is a frequent and well-known hazard on the south coast of England and anywhere up the east coast. On the east coast right up to Scotland the North Sea fogs are known as 'haars' and were a terrible problem to coastal airfields in that region when Britain was the unsinkable aircraft carrier for the allied air forces in the Second World War.

Coastwise fog is a met element that demands monitoring the shipping or coastal forecasts because land area forecasts will not usually be concerned with sea fog unless it is likely to come ashore. Even so in summer the deeper waters offshore are cooler than the coastwise ones and so fog is more likely offshore than along the coasts. In autumn, with sea temperatures at their highest compared to the land, sea fog is least likely, but in spring the reverse is the case. Then the water temperature is lowest compared to the land and fog will occur in airstreams that at other times of year would not be warm enough to produce any fog risk.

All this means that sea fog – which is perhaps the greatest hazard to small craft – is unpredictable. Only the general risk can be stressed and the mariner is left to assess the situation on the spot. If cumulus clouds build, if funnel smoke rises readily into the air, if the air really feels cool, forget fog risk. Think about the risk of fog when the air feels warm and rather muggy, when fuzzy lumps of low cloud begin to form or there is a lowish layer of amorphous cloud and when funnel smoke drops towards the sea. Use the glasses on the local shoreline because often the first place sea fog forms is where the air is lifted over the coast. It then spreads out to sea.

The final warning is simple. Stay clear of the shipping lanes when fog is likely to occur. Big merchantmen may be keeping a good look out and they may not. Their radar may pick you out of the sea surface 'grass' and they may not. The best place to be is certainly not where the bows of some supertanker may suddenly loom out of the murk above you.

22 When rain is forecast

Apart from the fact that it produces a wetting, rain is no great hazard to yachts. In fact a hefty shower may beat down a seaway and make it more manageable. It is what the rain means for the coming hours that is important.

Rain comes continuously and slowly when warm fronts approach. It comes suddenly and more-or-less heavily when cold fronts begin to pass and it comes in a mixture of these two modes when occlusions are involved. However, as occluded fronts are definitely old fronts, and are in

1 *The classic windy sky. This is jet cirrus in its purest form. Note how the fallstreaks trail rapidly back from the heads showing the strong change of wind with height – a typical sign of jetstream winds.*

2 *Nimbostratus (Ns) – the deep, dark rain clouds of bad weather.*

*3 The sun shines wanly through a veil of altostratus (As) and a few lumps
of stratus pannus (St pan) forming below show that it is about to rain.
Altostratus follow cirrostratus in the build-up to bad weather.*

4 *A front clears; we can see the break coming. Because the base is hard rather than amorphous this is probably an old feature, well past its prime.*

5 *Sometimes the advance of a cold front is invisible because of a total cover of low cloud ahead of it. At other times (as here) its leading edge with towering cumulonimbus (Cb) clouds can be seen. This could never be a warm front or an occlusion.*

6 *Cirrostratus (Cs), in which haloes appear, follow cirrus (Ci) in a deteriorating situation.*

7 *Fog patches sometimes envelope parts of the coastline leaving others in bright sunshine. Dense sea fog rarely shows such breaks.*

8 *Typical fair weather cumulus (Cu) over the sea. This is the kind of cloud that populates returning maritime Polar airstreams and the wind direction is often west.*

9 *The high level thunderstorms that occur in an encroaching front are often foretold by the small globular lumps of altocumulus floccus (Ac floc) or by long lines of cloud with or without turreted tops (Ac castellanus) that appear ahead. The sky often takes on a chaotic appearance.*

10 In the evenings of humid days the setting sun may be lost by developing
low cloud (stratus) which becomes total cover overnight, but is 'burned-off'
by the sun in the morning. This is a particular feature of coastal regions.

11 The 'battlements' of castellanus can be seen in the middle distance; the wind lies along these cloud lines. This is typical of the morning sky ahead of thunder later in the day.

12 When a cirrus sky shows no definite trends in direction or several directions appear crossing one another the winds aloft are usually light or contrary. This is only a bad omen when thunderstorms are possible.

the process of having most of their virility drained from them by subsiding air from above, so the rain from them will usually be less positive and may come in fits and starts.

Rainfall that is not frontal comes mainly from cumulonimbus clouds and a considerable proportion of summer rainfall is in the nature of heavy showers which may or may not be thundery as well. Thunderstorms undoubtedly produce the most prodigious downpours, particularly in the evening when storms, generated over the land during the afternoon, drift over the sea. There they lose their heat supply and the water in them, previously held in suspension aloft by the updraughts, cascades out of them as cloudbursts. While most rainfall does not impair visibility greatly, very heavy rain will certainly reduce it almost to fog limits.

The descriptions used in forecasts for different types of rainfall and the inferences that may be drawn can be read on page 62. Here we will just add a few comments that may be helpful in the longer term.

When a period of rain is forecast it is as well to try and divine from the general inference or in some other way what kind of front is going to be responsible. If it is a warm front the forecast rain itself is not a threat, but the clearance of the rain to fog, drizzle and low cloud that follows it can be. In a yacht you need hours of warning in order to make vital decisions as to whether to press on into the coming weather or to lay up somewhere while the worst passes. So when the clouds have built up in the way that warm frontal clouds do (see page 128) and the rain starts lightly (often with a light shower before it starts in earnest) and gradually intensifies without being in any way showery in nature, expect at least a couple of hours of rain, and often more, before there is any real fog risk. Fog, of course, follows the passage of the warm front and you can usually see where that is by the low trailing wisps of cloud (called virga) that stream along under the last of the rain clouds. You should also see a bright break coming behind, but that break is shortlived and the muggy wet airstream is usually quick to clamp down on ceiling and visibility.

The forecast should give some indication of how damp and fog-prone the air behind the warm front is likely to be. If its fetch is over mainly virgin sea expect the worst. If it is over a good length of land, especially hilly land, then mentally dry it out and expect better conditions. Here is where the actual weather reports can be useful. If Valentia and Scilly are both reporting bad visibility while it is still raining, but the visibility is not bad somewhere further east then expect the foggy conditions to spread eastwards and act accordingly.

If you recognize that you are already in the warm sector of a depression (see page 119) and a period of rain is forecast for later then it has to be some form of cold front as our knowledge of the structure of depressions leads us to expect that a cold front must eventually come along to put us back into the cooler Polar air that is our normal lot in these latitudes.

In this situation the forecast of 'rain later' warns of possible squalls as the front passes. It indicates a veer of wind as the frontal edge sweeps over you and that this may come even before the rain starts. It warns of possible thunderstorms along the line of the front, but it holds out the prospect of cooler clearer conditions where your recent worries about becoming fogbound will all disappear. Finally it suggests that by the end of the forecast period showers may well be your lot. However that will depend on where you are and what time of day it is. A cold front that clears across a landmass at evening will lead to a fine night whereas one that clears out of a northern sea area will almost certainly go on being showery by day or night. Showers behind cold fronts over the land will reach their maximum of intensity in the afternoon on most occasions.

With old frontal systems that are dying out, but still hanging around the sky as layers of relatively high altostratus or altocumulus cloud the rain may be of the occasional or intermittent kind (see page 62) and sometimes such old fronts can get new leases of life so that they suddenly produce lengthy periods of continuous rain. Or they may become unstable so that way above the mast (and only visible to airline passengers) great heads of cumulonimbus clouds will sprout into the air as if the cloud layer were a mushroom bed and the 'cunim' some vast fungoid growth. This is when thundery rain breaks out and thunderstorms with it. Possibly frightening, especially at night, as the cloud layers act like a sounding board and roll the thunder about in great reverberating peals. However such storms are less dangerous than the more conventional kind as most of the lightning jumps from cloud to cloud a mile or more above our heads.

Thus rain forecasts are helpful in assessing other, more important, weather effects in many instances and they should be carefully listened to for their wider inferences rather than for any more direct effects. There is, however, one direct effect of rain which is of great importance to cruising yachts. When rain falls it drags the air down with it. In this way air from way aloft finds its way to the sea surface when any form of moderate or heavy rain starts to fall. So the wind rises as the rain starts because the rain has brought down stronger wind from above. This effect is very prevalent when frontal rain commences and, added to the generally increasing wind to be expected as a low approaches, can make conditions worsen quite rapidly. It finds its most violent manifestations when major thunderstorms produce very heavy rain and/or hail. The intensity of the rain or hail is enough to induce violent 'falling' winds that spread around the storm edges and the wind rises in moments from light to 40 knots or more depending on the severity of the storm.

Finally, when the sky is lowering and darkening and it looks like rain, when will it actually rain? This is sometimes difficult, but there is one useful pointer. The cloudbase is often quite high when frontal rain is imminent. Under the true cloudbase fragmented lumps of dark cloud

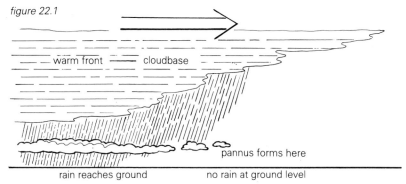

figure 22.1

warm front —— cloudbase

pannus forms here

rain reaches ground | no rain at ground level

When a warm front or occlusion approaches dark lumps (pannus) forming under the lowering cloudbase indicate that rain is very near.

called stratus pannus appear (pannus for short) and when you first see these rain usually occurs within 10 to 20 minutes (see figure 22.1 and photograph 3). As the rain grows in intensity what were odd lumps of pannus dotted around the sky grow more extensive and eventually, when it is raining steadily, they will cover the whole sky. Thus in bad weather the cloudbase you see is often not the one from which the rain is really falling. That is higher up and as the raindrops fall from some altitude they have time to lose some of their substance in evaporation. This saturates the air nearer the surface and the pannus forms in this wet air. Thus pannus is a sign of falling rain and often, at first, the raindrops may evaporate away before they ever reach the surface. However as the front advances so very soon the raindrops survive to the surface.

23 When thunderstorms are forecast

Thunderstorms are a phenomenon of the land rather than of the sea so often thunder over the sea started somewhere over the land. The most likely time for heavy thunderstorms is late afternoon or early evening and such storms often go on well into the night.

It would be useful to look at the comments on page 63 concerning the three main ways in which thunderstorms are described because not every forecast of thunder is going to produce the same kind of weather.

There are times when you expect thunder, but for most of the time you do not. Yet occasionally, when the weather is bad, you may hear a clap of

figure 23.1

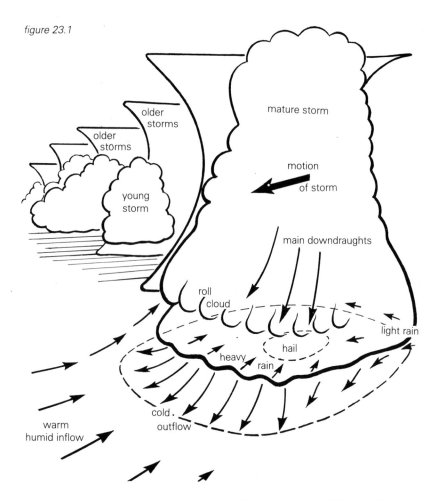

The anatomy of a thunderstorm system. Storm cells are old by the time they develop anvils.

thunder pealing through the sough of the wind. Such isolated storms are the sparse end of a spectrum that increases up to the occasional widespread outbreak that covers half the country and where the damage and casualties to life and limb hit the headlines.

We can understand the difference in storms when we accept that they are composed of cells that are born, grow to maturity and die. In the process they generate 'daughter' cells (apparently thunderstorms never have sons) which take over the role of the parents and in their turn go through the life cycle. Lifetime for a storm cell is perhaps half an hour in which time it grows to a peak of activity spewing out heavy rain, hail and lightning plus, of course, the consequent thunder (see figure 23.1). Then the cell dies away with light rain and its daughters, which have grown alongside it, take over. Thus even though the anvil is a recognition point for thunderstorms a cell with an anvil top is an old dying cell. It is the cloud with a growing cauliflower-shaped top that is in its prime producing hail and lightning and the anvils you can see around it or behind it merely point to the fact that the storm has been going on for a while allowing their anvil heads time to thrust up to great heights and so be forced to spread out under the tropopause.

The bad storms demand that there is very little wind at all altitudes because if the winds blow at widely different speeds through the decks of air in which the storm cells form, they will be torn apart before they can organize themselves. Thus big storms are found in shallow lows that may form part of moving pressure centres. Also they form in heat lows bred over the land by the sun's heating or in cols. The sight of a col on the weather map in summer should always make you think of thunder. Whether it occurs or not depends on several things, but the forecasters ought to give some indication of what thunder risk they feel is justified.

The storm cell idea explains that single cells can survive long enough to give a clap of thunder as a cold front races through in bad weather. The frontal storms have cells growing inside and through the cloud layers of the fronts on which they form. Cold fronts usually become thundery along their length and the storms pass relatively quickly whereas warm fronts and occlusions may develop a rash of storm cells spread over a wide area.

Both of the above types are due to air being lifted to levels where instability can set the air boiling up and no more heat is needed to fuel the storms. The heat storms have a different primary cause. They need a warm surface because they are just very large convection currents and again there are two kinds.

Scattered storms that grow here and there in a travelling airmass require relatively cold air to flow over warm sea or land. So they usually form in Polar air in spring when the difference between air straight out of the Polar stable and the sea isotherms is greatest. That does not stop them occurring at other times of year however. They are often described as 'airmass' storms – but not in forecasts. When storms develop it means that the air aloft is unusually cold because they are the most active weather elements that obey the heat seeks cold principle (see figure 23.2).

It may be difficult to realize that, as the sultry day waxes into the kind of heat that makes you wish you were afloat, the air aloft is colder than normal so that rising air never finds a layer warmer than itself and does not stop its upward flight until it hits the 'lid' of the tropopause and spreads out into false-cirrus anvils. Herein are necessary conditions for widespread and heavy storms that mushroom in prepared beds of low pressure which are more-or-less stationary.

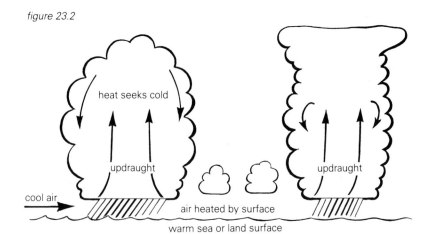

figure 23.2

How showers form.

Storms and Yachts

The sudden deluge of cold air that is brought down, anchored by friction to falling rain and hail, spreads around the leading edges of a storm cell as a dangerous squall. To yachts this sudden 'gale' just ahead of the storm edge is more likely to cause trouble than is lightning. For the worst of them the old saying about storms coming up against the wind is true, and, when the wind before the storm blows fitfully and hotly towards it, fear the worst (see figure 23.1). Lesser storms, and storm zones that have slowed up temporarily or permanently, spew out a moderate to fresh wind that blows from their direction, but the big ones suck their own wind towards them. To do that they need to be amongst the biggest and be travelling your way.

A typical wind change is from 5 to 10 knots towards the storm to a more-or-less sudden savage shift and increase to 30-40 knots away from it. The attendant drop in temperature, which may amount to 10°F or more, plus the gathering blackness and the growling and roaring of the storm, make for a highly unpleasant experience. The advice to be offered is equally unpalatable – sail off on port tack towards the storm and so beat through it. This is because of the slow speed of a yacht. The storm usually travels with the wind some 8000-10,000 ft up and if you can get sight of clouds at about this height (altocumulus clouds) before the storms strike try to gauge their direction of motion. It will be the most likely direction for the storms as well.

Having assessed that there is no other way and with the storm clouds stretched apparently unbroken across your path, you might think of running away from the monster. It is the worst thing you could do. Suddenly overtaken, as you would be as you beat slowly into the wind before the storm, by a gale-force squall from aft, you are a sitting target for a broach and knock-down. The subsequent panic might well lead to tragedy.

It may not be savoury, but the only way is to add your relative speed to that of the storm and so get through it as soon as possible by beating or close-reaching through it. As research shows that most big storms send out backed (anticlockwise) wind ahead of them so port tack is best at first. In the later stages, as the rain begins to lighten, the wind will also lighten and veer so that starboard tack is then best.

In the above we are assuming that the storm area is an active set of frontal storms or a widespread area of them with no sign of a break through which you could pass unscathed. It has to be pointed out that the sides of big storm cells is where they are most likely to grow daughter cells and so even an apparent break may be filled by a storm cell by the time you get there.

Obviously this advice does not apply to isolated airmass storms which are less vicious and whose effects are vastly more local. Even so I think experience will convince anyone not to trifle with the gusts and squalls that appear around any big shower cloud whether it be thundery or not.

This is not the place to go into details of protection of yachts against being struck. Incidentally it is remarkable how few yachts actually are struck and in a lifetime of interest in the subject I personally have only come across a handful of skippers who have had the experience. Even so when buying a yacht make sure that the mast is adequately earthed to the sea. This is of prime importance if the mast should step on deck. When a lightning flash strikes a masttop a vast amount of electric charge has to be dissipated. It will rush down the mast and if it is suddenly thwarted by having no direct path to follow it will build to an explosive potential so that moisture trapped in the wood at the base of the mast will suddenly conduct and heat. The resultant 'steam' blows the wood apart while the frustrated electric charge has to find some way to earth by sparking over to anything within its reach that is in any way connected to the sea. With a mast stepped on the keelson that may not be too bad, but if it should step on deck then members of the crew could be amongst the paths it selects. Of course rigging wires form the best path, but they may not be earthed themselves. Thus it is very advisable to see if your yacht is adequately earthed, with heavy metal straps where required, to something metallic and of sufficient area of contact with the sea. Incidentally a yacht fitted with an effective lightning conductor is less likely to be struck because one of the prime functions of such a conductor is to form an electric wind. This consists of a stream of ions from the masthead point which are of opposite sign to the potential in the base of the cloud. These will usually effectively lower the cloud potential and so prevent a flash occurring.

24 When fair weather is forecast

The word fair to the meteorologist means less than half cloudy for most of the time and no nasty weather. To the cruising yachtsman it means look out for coastwise windshifts due to seabreezes by day and landbreezes by night. Of course this presupposes that with the fair weather comes a lightish wind because local winds have great difficulty in starting up against moderate to fresh winds.

The typical fair weather day is one of blue skies populated by fleets of stately cumulus clouds that ride the wind like a bulbous set of flat-bottomed barges. Over the land the wind goes through its daily change of speed (the diurnal variation) gathering from minimum around dawn or a little after to become a maximum in mid-afternoon, falling light again with evening (see figure 24.1).

However this diurnal change is upset on many fair days in spring and summer because the wind pulls in to an on-shore direction as the day progresses so that an off-shore morning wind instead of going up progressively in speed goes down and may temporarily go to calm prior to picking up again as a seabreeze from seaward. The seabreeze strength however does rise to a maximum in mid-afternoon and then dies away with the onset of evening taking a clockwise shift as it does so. Thus many coastal summer evenings are either ones with next to no wind or a light

The daily variation in air and ground temperatures in summer. The curves may be adjusted in the vertical to allow for higher and lower maximum temperatures.

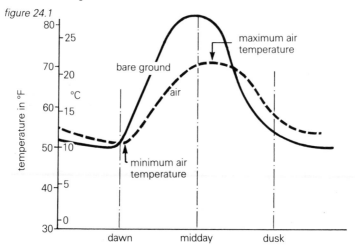

figure 24.1

breeze from the left-hand when facing the main coastline. In this connection read the more detailed comments in Sections 46 and 53 to further assess the prospects of seabreeze on any fair day and the general trend of winds to be expected off a coast with a particular orientation.

It is the pleasant light weather that often goes with fair conditions that is most prone to local wind variations and sometimes the reason for a wind that is not from the direction given in the forecast and is perhaps stronger or lighter than expected is difficult to find. Days with full sunshine develop heat lows inland. Thus a falling barometer in the middle of the day is to be expected in the heart of a landmass in summer. If that heart is not too far from the sea it can be fed by winds from the sea which blow in over all the coasts that look into the shallow centre of low pressure that is developing inland.

Such a closed centre is to be found over the Southeast Midlands of England where on average over the three hours 1000–1300 the barometer falls by 4 millibars or more on a warm, light weather day in late spring and summer (see figure 24.2). Over the adjacent North Sea and the Southwest Approaches there are similar tendencies for pressure to rise with time. Where such centres of rising tendency exist the air is sinking and flowing out. It flows out to feed the on-shore sea breezes that will tend to blow into the centres of falling pressure where the air is rising. The air that rises must perforce feed out at altitude to replace the air sinking over the sea areas. In this way a vast summer breeze system is set up.

It becomes monsoonal in character over the main landmass of Europe where the tendency is for air to flow southeastwards to feed heat lows over the Alps and the Balkan mountains. In looking at figure 24.2 we can think of the midday breezes blowing from the positive centres across the lines of equal tendency towards the negative ones. Where these lines are close together the seabreeze forces will be strong and where they are far apart they will be weak.

Thus there is a strong seabreeze drive from the North Sea on to the east coast of England and Scotland. There is a weaker one on to the west coast. There is a very strong one through the Skagerrak and across Denmark to feed the heat low over the Swedish mountains and the strongest of all is that over the coastal regions of Spain. The trend is weaker along the French Atlantique and Manche coasts, but makes up for its weakness in strength by its extensive fetch that only truly stops over the high land separating Northern Europe from the Mediterranean. It will be seen that there is an apparently strong trend for onshore breezes along the north German coastline, but many of these breezes start off as westerly or southwesterly winds and only later in the day do they turn to blow fully ashore.

The opposite trend at night is less marked and while the centres that were for sinking air now tend to become ones for rising air, so that the

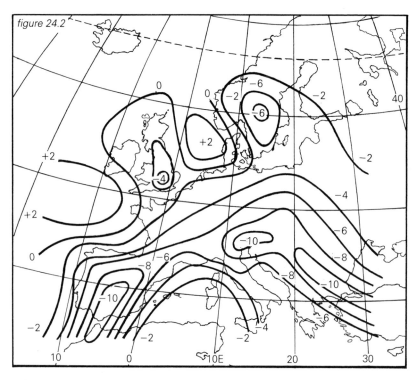

Where the air is mainly rising (negative numbers) and sinking (positive numbers) over Europe in the middle of the day in summer. The actual figures are the excess barometric tendencies ie over the North Sea +2 indicates sinking and outflow as the pressure rises while −4 over central England indicates inflow as the pressure falls. Thermal winds blow towards the negative centres and away from the positive ones.

night winds go the other way, most of the changeover is to small tendencies in the hours after midnight that in no way compensate for the strength of the daytime breezes. Here is the proof of the European summer 'monsoon' as more air flows ashore by day than blows back to sea at night. If the Continent appears, from the weather chart, to be hot then expect the daytime wind trends to be up the Channel and down the North Sea. Anticipate that this trend will be changed near the coasts to breezes that blow more directly on-shore. After dark expect the monsoon to go on, but more weakly and near the coasts anticipate off-shore nocturnal winds that rarely exceed 4–5 knots.

One result of all this cool moist sea air being hauled ashore is the eruption of inland thunderstorms that otherwise might not have occurred. Storms need to be fuelled and their working substance is water vapour.

However hot it may get, unless that water vapour is there storms will not occur. On the other hand the coastal breezes are perfect suppliers of the fuel for storms. Such storms not too far from the coast will initially enhance the on-shore wind strength and later kill it before reversing the trend to quite strong, cool off-shore breeze.

25 Pressure and the aneroid barometer

The aneroid (literally non-liquid) barometer is a very useful tool to carry on a small boat. It is robust and readings of its actual height need not be very accurate because it is the 'barometric tendency' that is important.

If you do not already possess a barometer and you are intending to buy one, try to get it calibrated in millibars (as well as inches of mercury if you like). The millibar (mb) is the standard pressure unit in use throughout the world and is much more wieldy than the vastly too large inch of mercury. The latter always entails a great deal of interpolation in difficult circumstances, but the millibar readings are much easier to see and use.

For scientific purposes standard pressure is 760 mm of mercury but this is usually high for most of the temperate latitudes: 760 mm = 29.92 inches = 1013.6 mb ie 1 mb is very close to 0.03 inches (about 1 per cent error).

An aneroid should be fixed under cover, but not in a confined space. For example in a battened cabin in a blow the barometer can oscillate considerably simply from pressure changes induced by the wind or sea battering on the hatches. This makes the actual reading difficult to take. However you may feel that there is no other safe place for the instrument than in the comparative safety of the cabin and you will put up with the variations that may ensue. Like all things you tend to get what you pay for, so within reason the more an instrument costs the better it usually proves to be. Shop around and even ring up and ask the instrument manufac-turers what might be best for your pocket and purpose before taking the plunge. You should make sure that the aneroid is a marine pattern specially designed for the rigours of life at sea.

If you decide you can afford a barograph you will be very disappointed in the performance of ones designed only to work on steady land. Unless the movement is oil-damped the trace will respond to rolling and pitching, pressure changes due to gusts and by the smacking of the craft when beating through a chop as well as picking up vibration when the motor is running. So if you intend to have the undoubted advantage of being able to surely identify when the pressure is beginning to fall then a marine pattern barograph is essential.

The scales on the charts (barograms) are not very open so the all-important first sign of a fall may well be masked by the other factors that are making the pen arm wobble. And it must be stated quite categorically that for foretelling coming bad weather a barometer is not as marvellous a device as it is cracked up to be. What the first signs of a falling barometer do is alert you to listen for a forecast or a gale warning, but you can pick up the intelligence just as easily with a simple aneroid barometer as with a barograph.

The reading of the barometer should be entered in the log every hour and the difference from the previous hour noted. This difference is the 'tendency' of the barometer over the hour. However the internationally agreed period for measuring tendency is three hours so if you ask a met office for the tendency they will tell you the difference between the barometer reading now and what it was three hours ago.

This is too long to wait when conditions are deteriorating at sea and so the small craft mariner's tendency can be considered to be the difference from an hour ago. With that criterion we can lay down some rough rules as to the wind speeds to be expected with certain tendencies. Obviously the steeper the barometer is falling the greater the wind that will accompany that fall. The problem, however, is that by the time the barometer is falling at a rate that signifies a gale there is just no time to make port except in special circumstances.

These are the tendencies that go with the higher Beaufort forces:

Fall per hour		Force to be expected
2 mb	0.06 in	6 (Yacht gale)
3 mb	0.09 in	8 (Gale or fresh gale)
6 mb	0.18 in	10–12 (Storm force or whole gale)

It is easy to see from this and your log entries when the barometer is falling at a dangerous rate.

Even so you must remember that if you intend to shelter it is no good waiting to see if the slow fall you now have will steepen into one of the above. Either you use the first signs of a falling barometric tendency as a warning, to alert you to other signs that can make the forecast of a coming blow more certain, or you can wait and use it as imminent intelligence of a wind that is about to hit you. In the latter case it will warn that gear must be secured and storm sails readied etc.

To this end I have designed the 'Gale Plotter' (see figure 25.1) on which the dangerous tendencies appear as lines of slope Y for a yacht gale, G for a full gale and S for storm force. Taking the pressure reading P at H hour

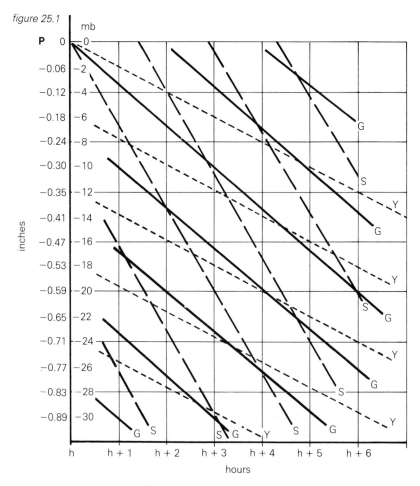

figure 25.1

The gale plotter. Using the readings from your aneroid barometer plot the fall of pressure hour by hour making the first reading P at H hour. Note down the actual value at H hour so that subsequent readings can be subtracted from it. The slope of the line that joins the plotted points at H and H + 3 hours is the standard 'tendency' of the barometer. If this approaches the steepness of the solid lines marked G a Force 8 gale is imminent . If it should fall more rapidly and approach the steepness of the lines marked S a Force 10, or more, gale is likely soon. In practice you can soon learn to gauge the steepness of the tendency that corresponds to the Beaufort Force in which you consider it prudent not to remain at sea. While the tendency is internationally measured over three hours should the barometer drop to the slope of the G line in a single hour read that as imminent warning of gale. The dotted lines marked Y are for a 'yacht gale' of Force 6.

and subtracting the value at H + 1, allows you to plot the slope over the first hour. You then subtract the value for H + 2 from H + 1 for the secónd hour etc. As the barometer falls more steeply you can begin to see when it is likely to achieve a 'gale' tendency.

However there are many smaller wanderings of the barometer which never result in a gale. Even falls that look as if they will become steep enough to bring a gale often flatten out later and even begin to rise. Undoubtedly the best use of the barometer is to give a visual indication that some trouble is possibly on the way. You need to add to that warning the much securer knowledge that comes over the airwaves and in lieu of a forecast know from the signs in the sky which encroaching cloud masses may bring strong weather and which will not.

26 Temperature

The internationally accepted temperature scale for met reports is the Celsius (Centigrade) scale. On this scale water freezes at 0°C and boils at 100°C under standard atmospheric pressure. However in Britain and America the Fahrenheit scale has been the domestic scale and continues to be so used. On this scale water freezes at 32°F and boils at 212°F. The latter scale while scientifically less acceptable has the advantage for domestic use that it does not go into negative values.

For those to whom Fahrenheit is the familiar scale the following table has certain mnemonic value:

Fahrenheit temperature		Centigrade temperature	Description
Below 32°		All minus values	Freezing
41°	(4+1=5)	5°	Cold
50°	(Both end in 0)	10°	Chilly
61°	(6,1 and 1,6)	16°	Mild
70°	(Ages of maturity)	21°	Warm
77°	(7=2+5)	25°	Hot
85°	(8−5=3)	30°	Very hot
95°	(Both end in 5)	35°	'Too hot'

The air temperature over the sea with a long sea fetch is very dependent on the underlying water temperature. If heap clouds grow over the sea the sea surface is warmer than the air. With sea fog or low cloud over the sea the sea surface is cooler than the air. Other conditions are more difficult to assess.

A yacht should carry a protected thermometer properly exposed out of direct sunlight and where it will not be subject to jarring or knocks. This will help to amplify the forecasts by showing when air temperature rises on passage of warm fronts or falls suddenly on the passage of cold fronts or occlusions. It may sometimes be difficult to recognize which kind of front is passing, or has just passed, and a thermometer will be an aid here.

Mercury in glass thermometers are usually the only ones that are going to be accurate enough for yachts at sea. The dial types that are to be bought from hardware stores and gardening shops are often hopelessly inaccurate. You might be lucky and get a good one, but you cannot be sure. Their simplicity and price may beckon, but go for the real thing even if it is more difficult to read. You can get good bi-metallic dial thermometers and these can be accurate. However buy such things from the manufacturers – you will rarely find them in shops.

Having said which, if your budget can run to it, there are remote sensing thermometers on the market that have a measuring head located on the outside of the hull and which will therefore give a constant reading of sea temperature sometimes in digital read-out. A sensing head can be mounted in a suitable place to also record the air temperature. With the two dials or read-outs side by side amongst your instrument bank you will be in a much better position to assess the possible sea-fog risks.

If all you can afford or wish to have is a mercury thermometer then if possible make it easily removable so that sea temperature may be taken in a bucket of recently gathered sea water. Sea surface temperature is very variable especially in coastal regions where there are shallows and drying banks and statistical values of sea temperature are not given here as they can vary very widely. The mariner should use his thermometer (or thermometers) to assess the difference between sea and air temperature when sea fog is forecast, but has not yet appeared. If the sea temperature is lower than the air temperature then fog is possible, but not certain. So we need the following criteria:

i Fog cannot occur when the sea temperature is higher than the air temperature. Signs include cumulus cloud over the sea which is not just drifting off the land, rising funnel smoke, relatively good visibility.

ii Fog is possible when the air temperature is higher than the sea temperature. Signs include sinking of flattened funnel smoke, relatively poor visibility even if no actual fog or mist is present. There are no truly representative cloud types that might suggest the likelihood of fog, but broken skies with high hazy cloud could occur before it.

The passage of warm fronts may change an area from situation i to ii and so the clouds of a front approaching may be taken as suggesting the possibility of fog in the outlook period.

Maximum and minimum thermometers and wet-and-dry bulb thermometers are of little use on yachts and should be avoided. They add little or nothing to a forecast.

Temperatures forecast for domestic radio and TV broadcasts are based on a process which involves recognizing the kind of airmass that will obtain at the time of the forecast and going through a complex process of deduction on a tephigram (see page 18). The descriptions used are based on statistical averages for the region in question for the season involved. Thus in Britain in summer (mid-May to mid-September) a day described as 'Hot' is expected to be 11°–14°F (6°–8°C) above the normal for the time of year. In spring (mid-March to mid-May) and autumn (mid-September to mid-November) a day that was 'rather cold' would be 3°–6°F below average (2°–3°C).

These 'sensation' descriptions will refer to people resting in the shade or doing light work. They do not allow for heavy work nor for any activity under the full sun.

Although shipping forecasts do not specifically mention temperature certain descriptions give inferences of it. Of these perhaps the description 'showers' is the most unequivocal. If showers occur over the sea the air is cool compared to the sea. When coupled with wind direction it can often be recognized that an airstream is Polar in origin and so one can expect the air to be cool or cold. Equally 'fog' or 'fog patches' indicate a relatively mild airmass with high humidity and again coupled with the wind direction it can be recognized that an airmass is Tropical in origin. However on most occasions the airmasses will not be as easy to identify from their weather descriptions.

27 Weather symbols

The international symbols for weather are as follows:

Rain	•	heavy rain	••
Drizzle	,	intermittent drizzle	‹,›
Shower	▽		
Thunderstorm	⟨		
Snow	✳		
Sleet	✻		

Hail	△
Fog	≡
Mist	=

Light and moderate rain are from a yachting viewpoint not very different; one dot will do for both. In the full reporting code the symbols are repeated in various configurations to show intensity and duration, but for our purposes it is sufficient just to double the dot for heavy rain etc.

Beaufort letters

The following letters are used to replace the above symbols and can give greater information. They are useful for your log. Small letters (r, p etc) for normal intensity become capitals (R, P etc) for high intensity while light precipitation is shown as r_0, p_0 etc. The letters are prefixed i for intermittent and repeated (r_0r_0, d_0d_0 etc) for continuous.

Rain	r	
Drizzle	d	
Passing shower	p	
Snow	s	
Sleet	rs	
Hail	h	
Fog	f	(visibility between 200 m and 1 km (200–1000 yds))
Thick fog	F	(visibility less than 200 m or 200 yds)
Mist	m	(visibility 1–2 km (1000–2000 yds) and obscuration due to water droplets)
Haze	z	(visibility 1–2 km and obscuration due to dry particulates like dust, smoke etc)
Lightning	l	
Thunder	t	
Thunderstorm	tlr	

Barometric tendency

The symbols used are designed to be a rough copy of the barograph trace. The standard period for tendency is three hours.

Symbol Pressure

/   increasing and then decreasing but pressure the same or higher than 3 hours ago

/   increasing then steady, or increasing and then increasing more slowly

/ increasing (steadily or unsteadily)

✓ decreasing then steady then increasing or increasing then increasing more rapidly

— steady

∨ decreasing then increasing, pressure same or lower than 3 hours ago

∟ decreasing then steady or decreasing then decreasing more slowly

\ decreasing (steadily or unsteadily)

∧ steady or increasing, then decreasing or decreasing then decreasing more rapidly

Wind speed and direction

There are two important, and different, methods. The first uses a whole barb for 2 Beaufort forces and half a barb for 1. The other, used on weather maps, employs half a barb for each 5 knot increase as shown.

Beaufort no	General description	*Beaufort force* Limits of velocity in knots	Symbol	*Knots* Limits of velocity in knots	Symbol
0	Calm	Less than 1	◎		◎
1	Light air	1 to 3		1 to 2	
2	Light breeze	4 to 6		3 to 7	
3	Gentle breeze	7 to 10		8 to 12	
4	Moderate breeze	11 to 16		13 to 17	
5	Fresh breeze	17 to 21		18 to 22	
6	Strong breeze	22 to 27		23 to 27	
7	Near gale	28 to 33		28 to 32	
8	Gale	34 to 40		33 to 37	

98

9	Strong gale	41 to 47		38 to 42	
10	Storm	48 to 55		43 to 47	
				48 to 52	
				53 to 57	

Sky cover

The sky can vary from being totally clear to being totally covered in cloud. The way of expressing the amount of sky covered by cloud is, by international agreement, in eighths of the celestial dome covered (oktas). It makes no difference how high or low the cloud is or if there are several layers, the observer assesses how many eighths are covered in cloud. The remaining eighths will be clear sky. A clear sky is truly what it says – not a cloud of any description. The merest wisp of cloud is recorded as ⅛ and the smallest hole in total cover brings it down to ⅞. When there is fog or very low cloud or dust or sand or even blowing snow make it impossible to see the true cloud above then 'sky obscured' is used.

Clear sky		Sky ⅝ covered	
Sky ⅛ covered		⁶⁄₈	
²⁄₈		⁷⁄₈	
³⁄₈		⁸⁄₈	
⁴⁄₈		Sky obscured	

These symbols are plotted in the 'station circle' on weather charts.

BBC TV symbols

Although they are designed to be self-explanatory the symbols shown on the BBC television weather forecasts need a little explanation in some cases.

	Temperature	Red figures on yellow ground for positive temperatures
(15)		Black figures on light blue ground for negative (°C)
	Sunshine	

Thin cloud or broken cloud but generally fair weather

 Thick cloud – possibly dull

 Sunny periods when the white cloud symbol is used but sunny intervals when the symbol is black

 Rain – mainly continuous

 Showers with sunny intervals or periods

 Snow and, with a sunshine symbol, snow showers with sunshine between

 Sleet

 Thunder or the possibility of it

 Wind speed (mph) and direction

FOG The word fog is written over the areas likely to be affected

28 Actual reports

There is nothing like knowing what the weather is actually doing at a position not too far away down your track. This is where actuals come in and you find there are not enough of them. The stations that are quoted are often not chosen for their representative qualities but for other reasons – like the fact that the best coastal station has closed down or is operating on a different schedule. You might think that Ronaldsway, the airport on the Isle of Man, was a perfect station for giving representative actuals for the Irish Sea. So it is, but it was replaced for a time by Blackpool airport.

In Britain the stations chosen to supplement the shipping and inshore waters' forecasts will do little or nothing to help decide whether seabreezes are blowing. This is because they are mainly at the wrong times ie outside the times of the seabreeze's day or they are for island sites or light vessels that may be beyond the fetch of the breeze.

Such drawbacks however do not preclude actuals being of great practical help as they represent solid information in a welter of forecast possibilities. If there is fog at Goeree then that is better than a forecast that fog is likely in the North Sea. Yet do not lose sight of the fact that no fog at Goeree does not preclude there being fog over extensive areas of the surrounding waters. An actual is only good for its immediate vicinity.

Actuals are broadcast for much of the North Sea by the Dutch station of Scheveningen. Scheveningen is an important station in that it covers a wide part of the coastal waters that are the frequent haunts of cruising yachtsmen from Britain and Europe. It broadcasts in English as well as Dutch and so caters for a wide spectrum of recipients (see appendix). Corresponding broadcasts by stations going northwards round the German Bight are also in English plus the host country's own language. The English arc extends throughout the Baltic. Southwards from Oostende all French stations broadcast wholly in French.

Imagine you are expecting a set-fair situation to break down and are trying to get an idea of where the invading depression is coming from. The barometric tendency at Valentia on the SW corner of Southern Ireland is a very useful one to note. If it is falling fast that fall may soon register on your own barometer further east and you are forewarned of possible trouble. However there are six full hours between one shipping forecast and the next and six hours is a long time in a changeable situation so the fact that Scilly had excellent visibility at 1200 does not mean that it is still clear at 1600–1700. Here is where a working knowledge of met comes in. You need to look around at other stations as well as having the weather map in mind to determine whether fair conditions are likely to be maintained. For example the good visibility could be because of sayings like *When the Lizard is clear rain is near* and a falling barometer at Valentia could confirm the onset of a low.

Actuals broadcast by countries of Continental Europe are often more detailed than those for Britain. The Swedes for example use a very dense network of actual stations round their coasts to provide instant information on the state of the icing of the Baltic etc and for those going to the Danish archipelago they also continue this network up the Kattegat.

Obviously a source of actuals is the telephone when ashore or R/T when afloat. You get to know which coastguard stations or coastal airfields etc are representative of your cruising area and it often helps to ring one of them before you set sail. Prestel (see page 28) is going to be a useful source of actuals in the future and other countries will have their own versions of such viewdata systems. Do not forget to add your own 'actual' to the broadcast ones, but remember that to make an adequate comparison you need to have noted the conditions you had two hours previous to the shipping or inshore waters' forecast you are listening to.

To use actuals to their fullest extent demands considerable met knowledge, but certainly when you listen to them their authoritative statements that the wind *was* SE Force 3, the visibility *was* good, the barometric tendency *was* rising slowly rather than falling quickly are very comforting bits of information.

29 Your own observations

As well as the forecast or actuals from coastal stations there is another very important observer to be consulted – you. You can see a sea horizon out to 3½ miles and in the clarity of the air before rain you may be able to see high cloud that is over 100 miles away. Those are not the theoretical limits which are:

Base of low clouds such as Cu and Sc – about 50 miles
Base of altostratus and similar medium level clouds – about 180 miles
Tops of thunderstorms and true cirrus clouds – 200 miles

In the above, the cloud elements have to appear low down on the horizon. However note that if a bank of cirrus cloud appears on the horizon then at jetstream speeds it can be over you in little more than an hour.

So you have an observation disc with a radius of 200 miles for high clouds invading a clear set-fair sky and a correspondingly smaller one for lower clouds. It is sometimes difficult to appreciate whether a cloudmass on the horizon is distant high cloud, or if it is sea fog, just over the sea horizon.

From your position you will know a good deal about the local situation. You will know:

i   if it is cloudy or not
ii if it is raining or not
iii what the visibility is
iv what oddities like thunderstorms or waterspouts the weather has produced
v   what the barometric pressure is (if you carry a barometer)
vi how the day feels ie is it humid or is the air relatively dry?
vii what the surface wind is

Using a shipping forecast blank you can plot this important observation at your position and add it to the actuals you have taken down from the forecast. You can then try drawing a few isobars, but as certain weather conditions occur with certain kinds of isobaric pattern when winds are in certain directions it is possible to get a hint as to what the weather map may look like in your vicinity.

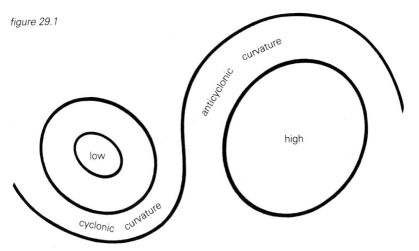

figure 29.1

The idea of cyclonic and anticyclonic curvature of the isobars.

The terms cyclonic and anticyclonic have not yet been covered, but are used in the following tables so figure 29.1 is added by way of explanation.

Hints on adding to the weather chart from your own observations (or from an actual). Sometimes the inferences given below will be wrong, but they suggest where the air is most likely to be coming from.

West to northwest wind

If the weather is	*Expect the isobars to*	*And to be*
Cool, showery	look back to northern seas	cyclonically curved (page 148)
Fair with Cu. Illustrated at A in figure 29.2	look out a long way into the west	straight or anticyclonically curved
Fine (little or no cloud)	form part of a ridge of high pressure	anticyclonically curved
Rain and/or drizzle (not obviously frontal)	form part of a nearby depression	strongly cyclonically curved
Frontal rain	form V-shaped kinks in the vicinity of the front	bent cyclonically – possibly extremely so
Thundery	form a cyclonic part of a col or a local low	cyclonically curved

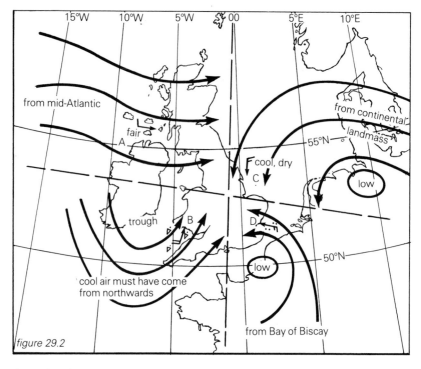

Assessing the run of the isobars from your own single observations of the present weather.

South to southwest wind

If weather is	Expect isobars to	And to be
Low cloud, drizzle, fog, muggy	look back on a long fetch to southern warm ocean	straight or cyclonically curved
Cloudy but mainly dry; visibility moderate	form part of the region between a low over the Atlantic and a high over Europe	mainly straight
Frequent passing showers. Illustrated at B in figure 29.2	have come round a local depression or deep trough to the west	strongly cyclonically curved
Thundery showers or thunderstorms	be associated with a local trough or perhaps the cyclonic side of a col	cyclonically curved or an area of slack pressure (if little wind)

South to southwest wind – continued

Cold and clear	form part of the circulation of a small high to the east. Could also be ahead of a not very active low or trough to the west	locally anticyclonically curved but straight or even cyclonically curved further back down wind

East to southeast wind

If weather is	*Expect isobars to*	*And to be*
Dry and bright and cool	look back into central Europe round a high over Scandinavia	anticyclonically curved or straight
Dry and bright and warm	look back round a low over Southwest Europe to the Mediterranean lands	locally anticyclonically curved but cyclonically curved further back
Dry and cloudy	form part of a low to the south	cyclonically curved
Wet. Illustrated at D in figure 29.2	form part of a local low to the south which is, or has been, in contact with the sea	strongly cyclonically curved
Showery and cool	form part of a local low closely to the west or southwest	strongly cyclonically curved
Thundery	form part of a heat depression over a land mass to the south	mainly weakly cyclonic but locally strongly cyclonic over the area of most intense activity

North to northeast wind

If weather is	*Expect isobars to*	*And to be*
Cool, showery	look back to northern seas	cyclonically curved or straight
Warm, dry	form part of the circulation of a low to the southeast or a high to northwest or west	more-or-less straight or anticyclonically curved

Fair	(difficult to comment)	straight or anticyclonically curved
Warm, humid	form part of a local high to west or southwest	anticyclonically curved
Cool, dry. This is illustrated at C in figure 29.2	look back round a low to the east where air is coming from the continental landmass	more-or-less straight with a tendency to cyclonic curvature
Frontal rain	part of circulation of a local low to the east or suspect an old front that has moved away from any low	cyclonically kinked in the region of the low
Rain and/or drizzle (not obviously frontal)	form part of a low that is quite close	cyclonically curved (probably strongly)
Thundery	form part of a local heat low (in summer). Otherwise thunder is rare with northerly winds	cyclonically curved

30 Plotting the shipping forecast

There are very few cruising yachtsmen who will start drawing detailed charts at sea from the information given in the shipping forecast but, having said that, there may be a great deal to be gained from learning a more-or-less self-evident code that enables you to quickly transfer the information on to a weather chart blank. The simplest way to describe such a code and how to use it is by giving actual examples:

Plymouth Biscay Finisterre Southerly 4 becoming southwesterly 5 or 6. Rain then showers. Moderate

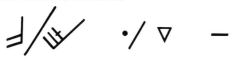

The oblique stroke signifies the passage of time. The small stroke on the fleche of the Force 6 arrow signifies 5 or 6. Moderate visibility is noted as a line. Rain then showers should make you think of a cold front or occlusion passing through the area during the period.

Rockall Malin Hebrides Southwesterly 3 becoming variable and later east or northeast 3 locally 4 in Rockall. Occasional rain later. Good becoming moderate

We need a symbol for 'variable' and the one shown is as good as any. Here we have three time periods; what it is now, what it will become and what it will be later. As occasional rain is later is will appear beyond the stroke and the rain symbol is placed in brackets to indicate that it is not expected to be continuous. A 'right' tick indicates visibility is good. Look up page 62 to deduce the finer points of the descriptions of rain.

Fastnet Southeast becoming cyclonic 4 and later southwesterly 5 locally 6. Rain at times. Moderate

We need a symbol for 'cyclonic' and an arrow circulating in the direction of cyclonic winds is about right. Rain at times is not significantly different from occasional rain to the mariner, but again page 62 will suggest the inference that can be drawn from the difference.

Dover Wight Portland Southwesterly 3 or 4 increasing 5 and occasionally 6 later. Occasional rain spreading east. Moderate locally poor

Here some simplification must be done. The higher force of '3 or 4' will warn of the worse to be expected. A stroke signifies later and 'occasionally 6' is evident from the Force 5 or 6 symbolism. The occasional rain spreading east symbol is self evident. Poor visibility is worth noting as mist and the 'occasional' brackets indicate that we are not to expect it everywhere. If they say 'on coasts' then you should draw the symbols on the coast.

Dogger Easterly 2 or 3 increasing 4 becoming southwesterly later. Rain at times. Poor with fog patches improving moderate later

Where no further speed value is quoted as in 'becoming southwesterly later' the speed is the last value quoted ie Force 4. Poor visibility is rendered by the mist symbol and patchy fog by the 'not-continuous' brackets while the moderate visibility symbol must follow the passage of time.

Cromarty Forth Tyne Mainly southerly 3 or 4. Showers. Moderate or good but coastal fog patches in the morning

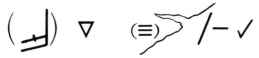

As the 'non-continuous' brackets cannot mean that for wind so we can use them in an allied meaning of 'mainly'. Coastal fog patches drawn on the coast with a stroke to indicate 'early'. The visibility symbols following the stroke indicate increasing visibility with the day.

German Bight Variable 2 or 3. Isolated thundery showers. Good

When the variable wind is given a speed you can add the fleches to the symbol. Thundery showers will be a shower symbol plus a lightning stroke and isolated in much the same as occasional although the meteorological meaning is different.

Humber Thames Southeast 3 locally 4. Showers, perhaps thunder. Good becoming moderate

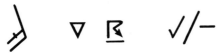

Locally 4 is not very important as it may occur where you are and it may not so indicate simply as Force 3 to 4. We need a means of expressing the degree of confidence felt by the forecasters so a horizontal line under a symbol indicates perhaps, possibly etc. Extend the degree of confidence with two lines for 'likely'.

108

Fisher Northwest 3 or 4 becoming variable 3. Mainly fair. Good

We need a symbol to indicate 'fair' and the international cumulus cloud symbol will show this well. The brackets again indicate not everywhere or all the time ie 'mainly'.

31 Notes on getting the forecast down

Once you are proficient in plotting and using the symbolism indicated on the previous pages (or some other symbolism that means something to you) it is best to plot the material straight on to the plotting sheet and not waste time writing it and then later turning it into symbols.

You can obtain the necessary practice at home from the radio or a radio-cassette recorder. Obviously the latter is better as you can go back over it as many times as you wish to iron out problems of phrases that are unusual. It would appear that in general printed plotting sheets as sold by yacht chandlers are too small and that too much space is given to a format to write the forecast down longhand and not enough to plotting the forecast straight on to the sea areas.

To overcome this it helps to draw your own by tracing a map of the Atlantic coasts of Europe (or any other area in which you are specifically interested). This should not be on a scale smaller than 1 in 5 million and it does not, for most purposes, need to go further north than 60°N. However it does need to go out into the Atlantic as far as possible (say to 25°W) and, if you can, as far south as 40°N. This is to pick up the positions of depressions that are going to come in from the direction of the Azores. In any other theatre of operations it is useful to read up about local depression tracks so that you can spread your chart in the right directions and avoid the frustration of not being able to plot the positions of incipient depressions.

An example is a depression mentioned in the shipping forecast for 0000 on 29 June 1974 which was put as '100 miles north of the Azores'. The Azores are about 38°N and 28°W and it is impossible to make a useful size of chart that goes so far into the southwest. However it illustrates the point that your perfect plotting chart will try to cover the zones from which the bad weather is likely to come. The work involved in making your own plotter is repaid when you can manage to plot the whole of a complicated sea area forecast without any hiatus because some important feature has been left off the chart.

Get to know the order in which the reports will come. In the case of British shipping forecasts they start in the northeast and work south and west before going back north. Draw a line connecting the areas mentioned to show that the report refers to all of them or ring the join of several areas. Anything simple to save a hitch. It is the problem of suddenly being faced with something unfamiliar that produces a mental block and militates against getting the forecast down. If what they say does produce a sudden mental block practise forgetting that and going on to get the rest down. To your own largescale plotter you can add the numbers or names of sea areas of other countries broadcasts to which you listen.

If you intend to plot the shipping forecasts it is certainly advisable to have a radio-cassette recorder with you so that you can get the forecast without having to sit and listen at a time which may be very inconvenient as you have to change tacks, change sails, even sup a bowl of soup while it's still hot.

The other practical point is that there are precious few modern sailors who are going to settle down in a Force 6–7 blow and start plotting detailed weather charts. That is inevitable, but unfortunate because it is just when conditions are most loaded against taking down the forecast that nature conspires to make it most imperative.

However there are certain points to be made here. You know the weather you have, and the actual reports from coastal stations will give you an idea of what it is like on other coasts. The actuals will warn sometimes of fog and their tendencies will help to confirm or deny the forecast of coming trouble, or better still, disappearing trouble, so the present state of the weather is not the most important thing. What would be much better would be a forecast of what things will be like some hours ahead. Thus if you intend to plot a simple chart plot the conditions forecast for the end of the period. Then watch the weather so that you can see how things are progressing with time.

Although it may seem complicated at first, the Metmap, originally designed for the Royal Meteorological Society by 'Wally' Wallington, but now also under the aegis of the Royal Yachting Association, allows plenty of space for plotting and writing down the information. However its format is such that the width of the British Isles is a matter of 3 in and you may find it rather too small. The Metmap is nevertheless excellent in most other ways giving amongst other things conversion of Beaufort force to knots, °C to °F, inches to millibars, lowest and highest sea temperatures etc plus geostrophic scales adjusted for the difference between surface wind speed and gradient wind speed. These help in moving fronts on, and as warm fronts travel slower than cold fronts or occlusions, there are geostrophic scales for these as well.

32 The station circle

Every meteorological station that reports is accorded a circle, called the 'station circle', over its position. The circles of any one country or region are numbered in a more-or-less systematic way with the smallest numbers in the extreme NW. The numbers increase eastwards and southwards.

figure 32.1a   *figure 32.1b*

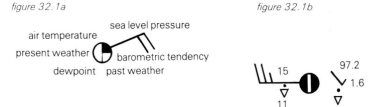

Examples of plotting simple station circles.

Each country or group of countries is identified by a geographic designator which in the region of Northwest Europe is 01 for Norway, 02 for Sweden, 03 for the British Isles, 06 for Holland and Denmark, 07 for France, 10 for Germany etc. Thus London Airport would be 03 722 to distinguish it from a station numbered 722 in some other region.

The full reporting code is complex and yields a very cluttered set of figures and symbols surrounding any station circle. Such complexity is only required by the professional forecasters. It is a positive menace to almost everyone else who just requires the bare bones.

The simplified plot shown in figure 32.1 tells us that the wind is W and 25 knots, there is ⅝ cloud cover, there are showers occurring now and in the past hour, the air temperature is 15°C and the dewpoint (the temperature to which the air must be cooled to produce fog) is 11°C. The barometric tendency is decreasing then increasing and the pressure is 1.6 mb lower than three hours ago. The atmospheric pressure reduced to sea level is 997.2 mb.

This is still too complicated for most purposes and on many charts designed for the use of the public only wind, cloud cover, air temperature and present weather are shown.

The mariner may need to use a similar plot when taking down actual reports from coastal stations. These will not usually include cloud cover, but will give the barometric tendency and the visibility. Visibility should be plotted where past weather is shown in figure 32.1a and the symbols for tendency are given on page 97.

figure 32.2

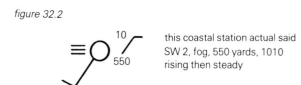

this coastal station actual said
SW 2, fog, 550 yards, 1010
rising then steady

Here Beaufort force is used and a long fleche on the wind arrow indicates two Beaufort forces. As we cannot have a pressure as low as 910 mb 10 must mean 1010 mb.

When ships make reports station circles are drawn round their given positions and the observations are plotted as for land stations, but with symbols for the direction the ship is steaming and its speed; and state of sea and wave conditions added.

33 Features of the weather map

Whether you intend to construct your own weather maps or not you cannot understand weather without being acquainted with weather maps and their features.

Isobars and the way they enclose centres of low and high pressure are already familiar so too is the idea that wind speed and direction can be measured from them. Symbols for station circle plotting and for writing down the shipping forecasts in a form of shorthand have been covered in the previous sections. The standard symbols for fronts have been illustrated and a good many of the features of weather maps have already been introduced.

An important feature not already covered is the col. A col is named after the saddle-backed region between two mountains and two valleys. In the met sense it is the 'saddle-backed' pressure region between two highs and two lows. In drawing weather charts cols often cause the uninitiated many problems. It seems so impossible to fit the isobars correctly.

The answer to this dilemma is to recognize that across a col the same pressure levels must look at one another, but the ones on the periphery of

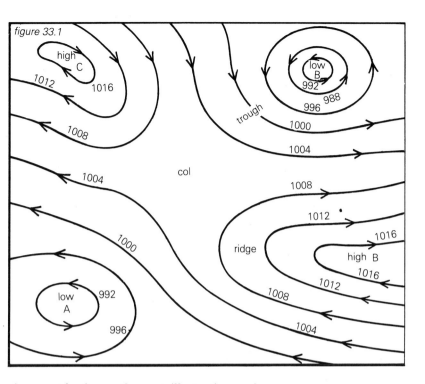

An example of a weather map illustrating a col.

the lows must be a step down from those round the highs. Once you recognize these simple facts drawing cols becomes much less difficult. In figure 33.1 the 1008 mb isobars surrounding the highs are well behaved and enclose their parent centres nicely. The low at the top is also easy to draw because where cyclonic isobars meet anticyclonic ones there is a natural progression of 4 mb steps from low to high as there must be. Also the wind directions tie up as they should do.

Undoubtedly the 1004 mb isobar at the bottom will be the most difficult to draw, but when it is realized that it must be part of both highs and the low (A) to the south it will become easier. As 1004 mb of the northern low (B) must look across the col to 1004 mb so the way it draws up is the only possibility.

Also illustrated in figure 33.1 is a ridge of high pressure and a trough of low pressure (other ridges and troughs besides those marked exist). It is sometimes difficult to decide, on a large area weather map with many features on it, which is a ridge and which a trough. I have personally always solved this problem with a simple mnemonic *Vees towards High mean a Valley*.

In figure 33.1 the trough marked has rounded V-shaped isobars sticking

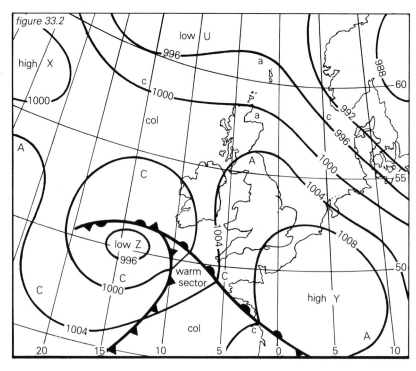

How to recognize cyclonic (C) and anticyclonic (A) regions of the weather map.

out towards higher pressure. It must therefore be a trough (or valley) in the isobars. Once the troughs are identified the features with opposite curvature must be ridges. Taking the 1004 mb isobar at the bottom of the figure as we move from right to left along it we first come to a weak ridge followed by a weak trough. The latter is easy to recognize from the mnemonic or, in this case, as part of the low. It may not always be so easy.

When looking at weather maps note the way the isobars curve. In figure 33.2 the regions of strong cyclonic curvature C are where weather will be worst because here is where air has to ascend, leading to cloud and precipitation. There are some strongly cyclonic regions around Low Z and across the warm front of this low there is a sharp 'vee' towards High Y so we expect that feature to be active there. There are two cols on this chart and the more northern one finds some slight cyclonic curvature c looking across at the strong curvature C. Showers occurring at c would not be very active whereas if they were occurring in the region of C they might well be big, squally and even thundery. This follows because cyclonic curvature worsens the weather where it occurs. Even slight cyclonic kinks will lead to increased cloudiness, if not rain.

114

Conversely regions of strong anticyclonic curvature A exist in the ridge from High Y that looks towards Low U. Equally following Low Z there is a marked ridge over the Atlantic where the cyclonic curvature is strong. Here our *Vees towards High* mnemonic might let us down as it appears to be directed at a High and so should be a trough. However it is obvious that as C is cyclonic the opposite must be anticyclonic curvature and real charts sometimes throw up oddities that at first sight do not fit the theories. However High X is a shallow feature and probably, if we could follow it through, the 1000 mb isobar round it is the same one crossing the chart above the col.

Isobars on the earth must be continuous. Somewhere on the globe an isobar has to make a closed loop. It is impossible to have an isobar that stops in mid-air. It is only the limits of our charts that make isobars discontinuous.

Another point to notice is how the symbols for the occlusion are reversed to show that the part on the right is travelling north while that on the left is moving south. Getting such things right helps in visualizing what will happen later as, in this example, the occlusion swings down behind the low centre as a 'back-bent occlusion'.

Next identify the airmass regions – if you can. One is easy. The warm sector between the warm and cold fronts must be fairly typical mT air (page 118) and so be a fog risk as it moves into the Channel. Fair weather in the Channel and North Sea now must give way soon to cyclonic weather with rain, drizzle and low cloud. It depends on how long the warm front takes to move to where your seat of interest lies.

To gain some clues lay the geostrophic wind scale (see page 151) over the isobars along the warm front. Take two thirds of that speed as the speed of movement of the warm front. It will give some approximate timing for the arrival of rain, poor visibility etc. All this hinges on whether Low Z will move eastwards or not. Only the forecast will really be able to tell you that.

If you can only draw a few isobars in your own area then extend the range of your prognostications using the clues given in Section 29. Together with the preamble to the shipping forecast, or some other forecast, it will help give you clues as to what the weather map looks like in your area.

Part Two

In the first part of the book we looked at forecasts and matters arising from them. Now in Part Two we will go into important aspects of the models we use in meteorology to explain weather systems and processes. In writing this I have been very conscious of the needs of the cruising yachtsman who is not destined to circumnavigate the world nor sail the Atlantic single-handed. Many things have been left out; for example, the processes by which precipitation (rain, drizzle, snow etc) comes about. It is not terribly important to know these things and it seemed better to use the available space for matters of more immediate concern to the practical sailor. No book can be totally comprehensive – and when it tries to be the average cruising yachtsman recoils in a state of mild shock at what is expected of him or her.

So in the following pages are the points which, after a long history of writing and lecturing for yachting people, I have found the important aspects of weather and wind as they affect the mainly coastwise cruiser. Difficult topics which can be useful have been relegated to an appendix.

34 About airmasses

The root cause of weather can be traced to temperature differences in the air. These, coupled with the amount of water vapour, bring about the attributes of airmasses and the zones that divide them one from another – the active regions we call fronts. We shall describe the attributes of fronts later, but the elements of temperature and humidity can be used to describe the basic properties of airmasses and these provide a vital introduction to the subject of weather.

To understand airmasses we must seek their source regions. These are places on the earth where there are permanent or semi-permanent anticyclones and the two main ones for Europe are the high pressure region over the North Pole and the similar one which exists over the

figure 34.1

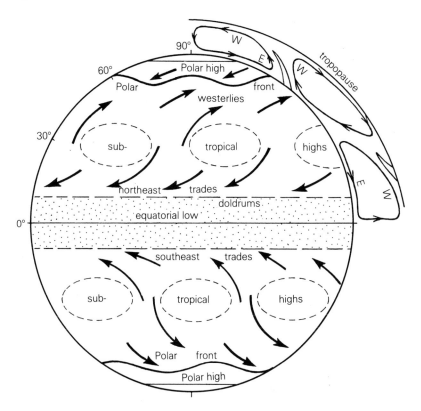

The major centres of pressure and wind of the world. The main upper wind circulations are either westerlies (W) or easterlies (E) and the arrows show the way the air rises along the main frontal system (the Polar front) and sinks over the great semi-permanent highs.

Atlantic between the Azores and America. In these anticyclones air sinks from high up in the atmosphere and this puts a kind of immense 'lid' on the air below. Under the lid air becomes slow moving, like all air in the middle of anticyclones, and it has plenty of time to acquire the temperature and humidity of the surface below it. Thus the air that stagnates over the Sargasso Sea becomes warm and wet through its whole depth and, as it originates in the sub-Tropics, is called maritime Tropical (mT) air when it is drawn out of its watery cradle and wafted northwards and westwards towards our shores (see figure 34.1).

Similarly the air that stagnates over the Pole becomes cold through its whole depth and it also becomes wet – though not as wet as the Tropical air. This follows because cold air has less capacity for water vapour than warm air. The resulting airmass is called maritime Polar (mP) and between them the mT and mP airmasses contribute a very great deal to our weather. Indeed in Britain and Atlantic Europe if you are not being influenced by one of these two airmasses conditions are not normal.

However not all mT air is going to be as perfectly wet and warm, or mP air wet and cold, as it originally was because the weather charts are covered in fronts separating airmasses that have spent a long time gyrating round the North Atlantic theatre of weather operations. In so-doing they have usually been acted on by two modifying effects:

i near the surface they have acquired the attributes of the land and sea surfaces over which they have travelled since leaving 'home' in the permanent anticyclones
ii they have suffered from air subsiding on to them from high above and so have become layered and stratified in a way they were not when fresh from the Tropical or Polar stable

Allowing for these modifying influences it is best to describe the basic recognition points of the main airmasses that affect us. Once the attributes of the airmasses at their purest are known you are in a position to recognize them for what they were even when they have been substantially modified. But before we can set down a table of airmasses there are two other main ones to be considered. These are the Continental airmasses whose main distinguishing feature is their dryness.

The dry, warm airmass that affects us is called continental Tropical (cT) and its source may be over North Africa. It comes on southerly and particularly southeasterly winds and needs to have travelled most of the way over land so as not to pick up water vapour. However when it does pick up moisture it can be quite humid even when clouds do not form in extensive amounts. This is an example of a modified cT air.

The dry cold airmass comes from Central Northern Europe or Scandinavia, and in winter from the great Siberian Anticyclone. As the latter encloses the greatest quantity of cold to be found on earth so continental Polar air (or sometimes Arctic air) is the stuff of which our hardest winters are made. At other times of the year, when the Siberian high has declined and spread right down through Central Asia to cover Asia Minor, Southern Russia and Northern India, cP air is cool and dry and often quite clear.

Between them these four airmasses provide the bulk of our weather and here is a summary of their attributes:

Abbreviation	Name	Typical weather	Source
mT	Maritime Tropical	Extensively cloudy with rain and drizzle. Poor visibility and fog	Azores High

mP	Maritime Polar	Showers and bright periods. Good visibility	Polar High
rmP	Returning Maritime Polar	Cool but fair. Good visibility	as mP modified by Atlantic Ocean
cP	Continental Polar	Intensely cold and often cloudy in winter	Siberian High
cT	Continental Tropical	Very warm and cloudless	Southern Europe or N. Africa

It follows that the first, most important, question to be answered when starting to do your own weather forecasting is 'What airmass am I in?' There is often no doubt about the answer as when the cold showers blow in on the NW wind. Then you are certain you have mP air. Or when low cloud drives by apparently not far off the masthead, it feels muggy and the visibility is much less than you would like. You have no doubt then that the airmass is maritime Tropical. However when the wind is west and Force 3 to 4, the visibility is good and fair weather cumulus clouds drift over between the blue breaks, what then? The airstream is now what is called returning maritime Polar (rmP) and should not prove a problem as it has the basic attributes of a Polar airstream ie good visibility and cumulus clouds. The fact that the cumulus is now humble stuff compared to the great cumulonimbus of a pure mP airmass is due to a past history of a long sea track and of immense numbers of showers that grew and died over the wastes of the Atlantic in the days following the extraction of the airmass from its Polar source. These served to take the warmth of the sea surface aloft and so established a warm layer (an inversion) over the surface airstream which prevents the cumulus clouds from growing. The result is fair weather Cu (see figure 34.2 and photograph 8).

Returning maritime Polar air is just one prevalent example of a modified airmass, but the sight of a weather chart, together with the well-known truism *The air behind a front gives its name to the front*, will usually indicate what kind of modified airmass you are in. Expect such airmasses to have developed two or more decks with different attributes. In such decks clouds may grow or they may disperse. When old fronts are in the offing layers of clear air may appear between cloudy zones above and below them. In older mT airstreams, that have dried out with time, many different layers of clouds, including high clouds (cirrus), medium level clouds (like altostratus or altocumulus) as well as low clouds, will be seen. The latter would be a total cover in a fresh, pristine mT airmass, but in the modified one there may be large clear areas into which low clouds occasionally drift and in which, particularly overnight, a complete layer of

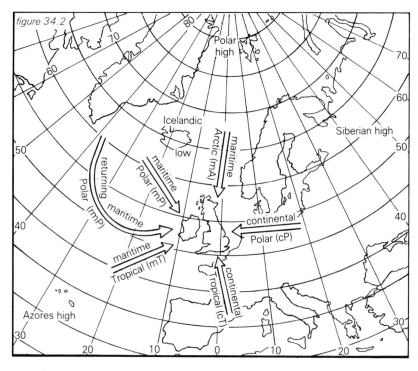

The directions from which the airmasses approach Britain.

low stratus cloud may possibly suddenly build. You have to recognize such airstreams by attributes like unnatural warmth and humidity, plus considerable cloudiness of the layered variety whereas a Polar airstream will not be half as cloudy aloft (see photograph 10).

35 Facts about depressions

Depressions are in effect atmospheric heat engines deriving their energy from the temperature contrast between their parts and so the most vigorous depressions tend to be associated with unusually warm and cold airmasses. They are also regions where air is mainly rising and so cooling, from which it follows that cloud and precipitation result. This is in contrast to anticyclones where the air is mainly sinking and warming, so leading to the erosion of cloud and the suppression of any form of precipitation.

Most depressions (lows) form along the Polar front in mid-Atlantic and so are called Polar-front depressions. Other kinds of low include:

i heat lows, that form over land in summer

ii Polar lows, which wing down from northern seas. They are frontless whirls of cold, wet air in which unseasonally cold showers frequently occur. Undoubtedly some of the most depressing weather comes with Polar lows

iii wave lows, which are embryonic frontal depressions that do not develop. They temporarily deteriorate the weather and cause the fronts on which they form to produce more rain and cloud for longer than they otherwise would

iv old hurricanes that rejuvenate on approaching Atlantic Europe, especially the Southwest Approaches. These are phenomena of autumn, but they occasionally produce extremely intense blows in the west of Britain and Ireland as well as affecting the coasts of Atlantic France

Polar front depressions are by far the most prevalent. They tend to form in families over the Atlantic following a period of anticyclonic weather. The waning of the Atlantic high allows the Polar and Tropical airmasses to again war with one another and each succeeding depression formed comes further and further south. Eventually the cold air penetrates into the Mediterranean and the cycle is broken, usually by another spell of anticyclonic weather.

However it is a well-known feature of the weather map that there is often a more or less stationary (quasi-stationary) low to the south of Iceland which acts as a kind of melting pot for the Atlantic depressions that curve into it and are swallowed by it. When such a depression sticks off the northwest coasts the resulting weather is cyclonic for days with rare glimpses of the sun and a constant threat of rain or drizzle. Extensive periods of dull weather in summer are usually due to quasi-stationary lows which are not too far away from the scene of the weather experienced.

Depressions follow the rule *Size times speed of movement tends to be constant*. Thus great sprawling areas of low pressure are almost stationary and just tend to heave about their main centres sometimes making peripheral sea areas more-or-less cyclonic. At the other end of the scale are the wave lows which often run at great speed (as much as 60 knots) along parts of the Polar front. The main mass of depressions fall between these extremes. Young ones, whose circulations may not extend above about 10,000 ft (3 km) tend to travel fast, but as they get older and bigger they tend to travel more slowly. Eventually many depressions may end up almost stationary over Scandinavia.

Another useful rule of thumb is *A depression that moves will not deepen while one that deepens will not move*. Here we have to read the spirit of the statement and not take it too literally. It is based, however, on conservation of energy. If the depression is using energy to travel it is far less likely to be able to deepen and become more intense. Many lows which start off moving quite fast without deepening may develop the conditions that allow them to deepen. They will then usually slow up. Thus if the forecast indicates a depression is slowing up ask yourself 'Will it therefore deepen and create worse weather?' As an example the low which caused the Fastnet storm of August 1979 travelled rapidly across the Atlantic without appreciable change of pressure then, when it started to deepen on approaching the Irish coast, it also slowed up.

Lows which approach Europe from the Atlantic have been classified, but the classification is not of great practical use to yachtsmen. Suffice to say there are lows which curve down into the North Sea from south of Iceland and they can be vigorous. We have already mentioned another category – the families of Polar front depressions. These tend to track straight across Britain in a more-or-less northeasterly direction, but late members of a family tend to steer for the English Channel and use it as an entry to Europe, producing long hours of rainfall in the area and often showing a reluctance to forsake the water for the land. The 'Channel Low' is a pretty prevalent beast and some of the Channel depressions can be very nasty indeed even in the height of summer when quite innocuous-looking wave lows have at times deepened along the French coast and created survival conditions in the waters of the Channel Islands.

A typical year finds some 150–200 lows crossing Britain somewhere and of these perhaps 50 per cent are Polar front depressions while young secondary depressions which form in the circulations of the others account for a further 30 per cent. The latter are of importance to the mariner as they tend to form near Britain and so are vigorous and fully engorged with moisture to form deep clouds and much precipitation. Polar lows account for a sizeable chunk of the remainder, but to the total must be added the heat lows and other odds and ends such as the not-very-prevalent depressions that track from Iceland into the North Sea.

36 The life history of Polar front depressions

Most depressions start as 'waves' on the Polar front (see figure 36.1). The Polar front is the line of division between warm, humid Tropical air and cold, humid Polar air that sometimes stretches in an almost unbroken line

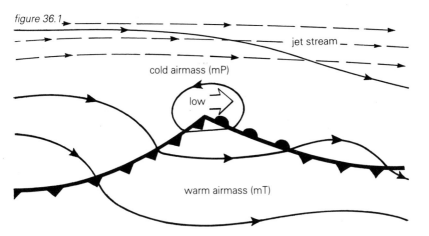

figure 36.1

cold airmass (mP)

low

jet stream

warm airmass (mT)

Depressions start off as wave lows to the south of the jetstream.

for thousands of miles across the Atlantic. Not all waves develop into full-blooded depressions as depressions need over 1000 miles of undisturbed front in order to develop their full potential. If they are not given the necessary space in which to grow they will run fast along the Polar front bringing temporary deterioration to places in their path, but no very strong winds. It is the wave that deepens which will produce gales.

One of the primary factors in its development is the position of the wave with respect to the jetstream that will be found 200 or more miles to the north. Jets and developing depressions go together and you cannot have one without the other. Where the surface frontal lines, the air masses and the jet will lie, when a young wave is going to develop into a vigorous depression, is shown in figure 36.2 while figure 36.3 shows a cross-section of a typical strong jet. A skeleton of this diagram has been raised above the warm and cold fronts in figure 36.2.

Assuming that the wave develops it will, after a period of a couple of days or less, transform into the kind of system shown next. It will, as far as we are concerned, have become a 'model' depression (see figure 36.4).

A model depression has the following features:

i a centre of low pressure, encircled by
ii rings of isobars which roughly show the wind direction

The airmasses essential to the life of the depression are, at the surface, split into three zones by lines of division or fronts. There is usually:

iii cool air ahead
iv cold air behind
 v warm, humid air in the warm sector

figure 36.2

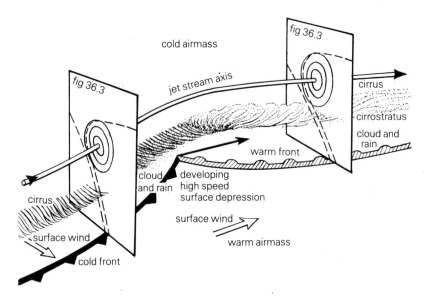

A three-dimensional view of where a young depression will develop. The jet, depicted as round because of the scale of the diagram, is really a flat tube of high speed winds. The cross-section of fronts and upper winds (fig 36.3) fits over both warm and cold fronts as shown. Only cirrus and cirrostratus clouds are suggested.

The low tends to move in a direction:

vi parallel to the isobars in the warm sector and at a speed that is variable, but tends to fit the rule

vii the smaller the low the faster it moves

The low centre exists to the south of a jet stream when the depression is going to continue to develop. How to recognize the presence of a jet from the clouds that accompany it is covered in Section 41. Recognizing that a jet is there is important to the mariner in the path of a forecast low because it will indicate that the low is deepening ie developing and is likely to produce gale-force winds.

Above right: How the upper winds, the frontal zone and the jet fit together. The speeds are typical for winter and can be reduced somewhat for summer.

Right: A model of a developing depression.

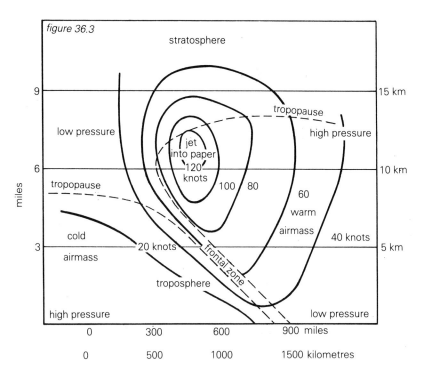

figure 36.3

stratosphere

9 — 15 km

tropopause

low pressure — high pressure

6 — 10 km

jet into paper

120 knots 100 80

tropopause

60 warm airmass

cold 40 knots 5 km

3 — 20 knots frontal zone

airmass

troposphere

high pressure low pressure

| 0 | 300 | 600 | 900 miles |
| 0 | 500 | 1000 | 1500 kilometres |

miles

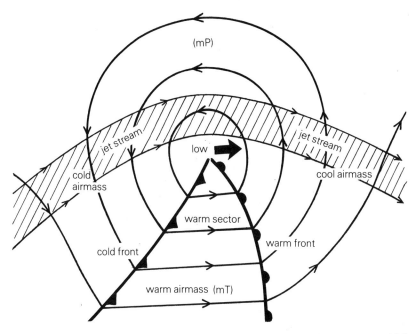

figure 36.4

(mP)

jet stream

low

cold airmass

warm sector

cool airmass

cold front

warm front

warm airmass (mT)

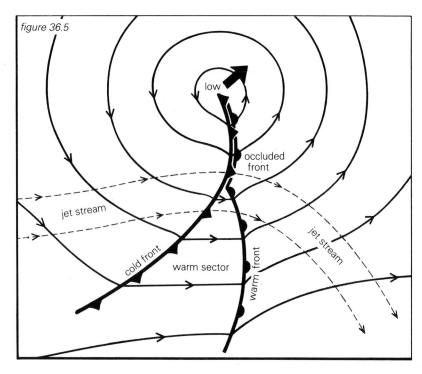

A typical example of an occluding depression.

After some days the travelling low will begin to occlude (see figure 36.5). In this case:

a the low centre may be in the relative position shown or
b it may move down the occluding front so that the latter bends back through it (a back-bent occlusion)

In either case the warm sector is squeezed out progressively leaving no warm airmass on the ground.

An occluding depression is past its prime and is filling. Its centre will move through beneath the jet stream to keep the point of occlusion under the jet. Thus old lows are found north of the jetstreams and new developing lows to the south of it.

37 Facts about fronts

Fronts form wherever two dissimilar airmasses come into contact (see figure 37.1).

The exact details of how that happens are not important to the practical sailor because by the time the fronts get to Britain and Europe they are already formed. So while the situation depicted in a must happen out on the Atlantic somewhere it is situation b that is of practical importance.

Because of the difference in densities of the warm and cold airmasses at all heights it is certain that the surface between them must eventually slope. The slope may not be as regular as depicted, but it has to be there. Because of various factors the slope of a cold front (typically 1 in 25) is about twice as great as that of a warm front. In practical terms this means that a cold front clears in half the time a warm front takes to clear.

The tropopause is lower in the cold air than in the warm and the jetstream snakes through the cold upper air near the point of discontinuity between the different heights of the tropopause (see figure 36.3). The tropopause is not something that is physically detectable from the ground. It occurs where the normal situation of temperature falling progressively with height is suddenly transformed into a zone where temperature is constant. Under this zone are formed all the clouds and weather in which we are interested. From that point of view the tropopause is the 'top of the atmosphere'. The highest clouds you see are under the tropopause which is a little higher than the highest cirrus. It is also revealed by the anvil tops of the biggest cumulonimbus clouds pressing against it.

The vast masses of cloud and attendant rain that form above frontal surfaces, whether they are warm or cold fronts, come about because of

Schematic diagram of how a frontal surface forms. In (a) the two dissimilar airmasses have just come into contact. The inevitable result (b) must be that the surface of contact develops a slope.

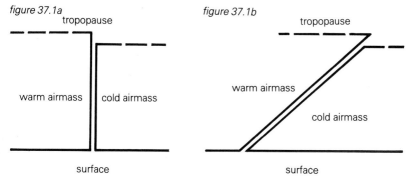

figure 37.1a
tropopause

warm airmass   cold airmass

surface

figure 37.1b
tropopause

warm airmass

cold airmass

surface

lifting. The way the warm air is lifted over the cold means that the air cools in bulk and, being already overloaded with water vapour, condenses into cloud. Further lifting generates the rain processes. Along cold fronts a showery rain-making process adds to the more gentle 'lifted' rain. As warm fronts are rarely showery this can provide a means of detecting that the front you have is in fact a cold front and not another warm front. The showers, embedded in the layer clouds of the front, are precipitated by the very rapid lifting when the cold air behind the front drives in under it. Thunderstorms may even occur due to this process.

Warm Fronts

Because the warm frontal surface slopes up over the cold air ahead of a coming depression by many hundreds of miles its characteristic clouds forewarn of coming bad weather. Therefore the mariner intent on keeping clear of trouble learns to recognize the sequence of clouds that appear above him as the front encroaches.

So, as in figure 37.2, the first cloud to appear is cirrus (Ci). The initial forms will include hooked cirrus (photograph 1) which may be 500 miles and 12 hours ahead of the point where the warm front will clear and introduce the muggy-warm air of the warm sector. Before that happens the cirrus will thicken across the sky and eventually be replaced by cirrostratus (photograph 6) that forms a halo about the sun or the moon. In its turn this will thicken into altostratus which will be thin at first, but into which the sun will gradually disappear as if going behind frosted glass (photograph 3). As the warm air wedge deepens several miles above your head the sun will go completely and, in its purest form, the altostratus will gain the appearance of dark blue-grey mudflats with very few features. Rain may begin to fall from this cloud, but it will not usually reach the ground, because it evaporates on the way down. In doing so it saturates the airspace below the cloudbase with water vapour. This causes a special form of stratus cloud called 'pannus' to form (photograph 3). This is easily

A cross-section through a typical ana-warm front in its prime.

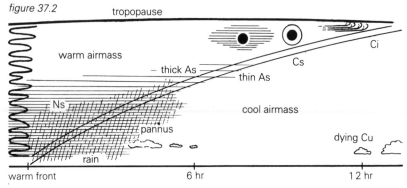

figure 37.2   tropopause

warm airmass

thick As
thin As

Ns

cool airmass

pannus

dying Cu

rain

warm front   6 hr   12 hr

Ci

Cs

recognized as dark lumps of misty cloud populating the airspace in increasing amount and from a practical point of view signifying that it is time to don an oilskin and move things below.

Very soon after pannus begins to appear the real rain comes, slight at first, even intermittent in character. Gradually, however, with time the rain increases in intensity, but with the model warm front it should not be showery in nature. At the same time the pannus grows to cover the sky at a low level driving by on the wind which also must now be on the increase. The cloud from which continuous rain falls is nimbostratus (Ns) (photograph 2) and you should expect a few hours of rain. Thus, to recap, the cloud sequence that extends along a coming warm front (or occlusion) is:

Cirrus – mare's tails
Cirrostratus – haloes
Altostratus – disappearing sun
Nimbostratus – rain

The times given on the diagram are typical but sometimes a front takes longer to pass than this and sometimes it passes more quickly. The time referred to here is from when you first see the cirrus to when it clears at ground level. A useful rule of thumb is *The time interval from cirrus to losing the sun is about the same as from losing the sun to when it rains.*

So if you noted in the log when you first saw the cirrus of a coming front and found the time to when the sun finally disappeared into the deepening grey clouds you could expect the rain to commence after that same interval later (ie three hours from Ci to loss of sun so another three hours to rain). It does not always work, but in lieu of any other indication it can be a useful rule. We have to remember the old adage with regard to weather (including fronts) *Long foretold – long hold; short forecast – soon past.*

When a warm front passes

The signs that a warm front is passing (photograph 4) include:

  i gathering light on the windward horizon as it approaches
 ii a very low cloudbase with dark trailing wisps of fracto-stratus hanging beneath just as it is about to clear
iii a break from rain and total cloud cover to broken cloud as it moves away. Look for the tops of the cloud following the front; they should not be very high. If they should tower the front is probably an occlusion or some form of cold front
 iv a veer of wind from SW to W or perhaps S to SW as the front passes
  v a kick-up in the barometer reading, but not a significant rise. If the front clears as above and the barometer continues to fall allow for much stronger wind to come
 vi a rise in temperature and humidity. It may well feel muggy-warm

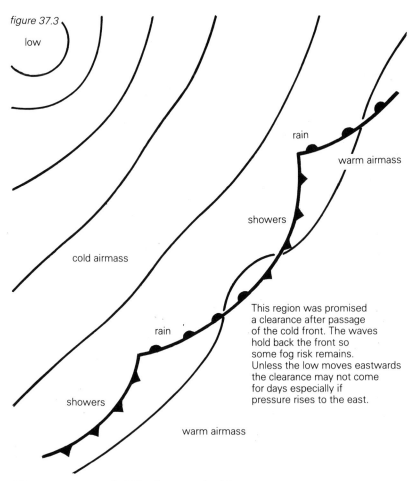

How waves act to hold back a promised front.

vii after a brief spell of broken skies just behind the front expect low
cloud to close in with drizzle or more rain and very poor visibility

All or some of these attributes may be present when warm fronts pass.
And:

viii if a warm front (or occlusion) has produced a fair quantity of rain, but
the wind has not risen much then expect the wind to rise later (*When
the rain's before the wind then your halyards you must mind*).

Weak fronts

Not all warm fronts are the same. The one described above is the kind
called an 'ana' warm front where all the air is rising (*ana*: Greek, up), but
many fronts that cross Atlantic Europe are only ghosts of a once proud

'ana' past. These are called 'kata' fronts (*kata*: Greek, down) because over them air is sinking and eroding the higher clouds that they once possessed. You may not be aware of this from the ground as the clouds near the surface are often the last to be eroded and the total cover makes it impossible to see what is happening above. However when, in the cloud build-up of a front, there seem to be big spaces appearing in encroaching high clouds suspect that the front is an older one. This means it could well be an occluded front with no warm sector. The practical outcome of that intelligence is that there is little or no fog risk such as would occur in a warm sector.

When a front is forecast sometimes, ahead of it, an unsuspected amount of rain will fall from another old front that no-one knew was there. Whenever the rain breaks out much earlier than the forecasters thought suspect that the real front is yet to come.

The last dying gasps of an ancient warm front are usually experienced as a period of increased cloudiness from which some light rain or drizzle falls, but the front has normally lost all touch with the depression with which it originally formed. Such fronts will not make the weather deteriorate very greatly, but it cannot be forgotten that old fronts can get new leases of life and it is not unknown for it to rain for hours or even days from an old front that has got ensnared in some isobars that are lying almost parallel to it. Fronts that end up along the isobars rather than across them are candidates for the formation of small waves (see figure 37.3). The waves will not produce much wind, but they can induce a great deal of rain and as fronts like this cannot move much it remains nasty for a long time.

38 Cold fronts

These are warm fronts in reverse, but they are usually more active than warm fronts. Figure 38.1 is a cross-section through an ana cold front ie a cold front in its prime.

The passage of a cold front (photograph 5) will:

a usually be accompanied by low cloud and heavy showers
b often be preceded by a break in the cloudiness of the warm sector
c cause the barometer to kick up
d produce a marked drop in temperature
e often produce a sharp veer (clockwise shift) together with a confused cross-sea
f sometimes be accompanied by squalls or even thunderstorms

figure 38.1

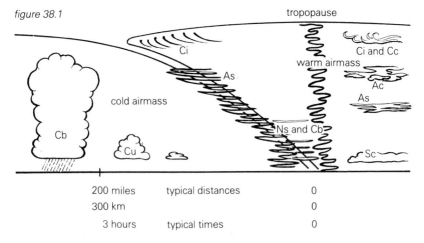

200 miles	typical distances	0
300 km		0
3 hours	typical times	0

Cross-section through a typical ana-cold front.

In the cold air, as the front clears away, the cloud sequence seen ahead of the warm front occurs, but in reverse order. There will be:

i nimbostratus with cumulonimbus (shower clouds) mixed in with it. The latter are not characteristic of warm fronts (although showery and thundery warm fronts do occur)

ii a clearance of the rain as lifting tiers of altostratus stretch above the observer to be followed by

iii cirrus whose fallstreaks point down towards the retreating warm airmass (it is rare to have haloes about the sun or moon for more than a brief time when a cold front is clearing unlike the same phenomenon with a warm front where haloes may persist for a couple of hours or more)

As the front clears the windward horizon will first of all seem rather clear of cloud but, as the cold air deepens behind the front, first cumulus, and then cumulonimbus clouds leading to showers, usually develop.

The intensity of showers that result behind a clearing cold front depends on how cold the air is and how warm the sea or land is. The former will not change its temperature during the day, but the latter will. Thus over the sea, in the cold Polar air that streams in behind a retreating depression, showers will often occur by day and night without much difference between the daylight and dark periods. Not so over the land where the heating of the land by day leads to maximum showers in the afternoon and minimum showers overnight. The showers usually die out over land as soon as the sun sets and so if off a leeward coast this diurnal pattern will occur whereas off a windward coast, which looks out into the ocean, showers are possible at any time of day or night.

However, even over the sea there are times when a batch of showers can be followed by a more-or-less long period with few if any. Such events are due to different compositions of the airdecks above which either, by their characteristics, encourage shower clouds to grow or inhibit their growth. The situation is similar over the land and far from windward coasts the tendency is for showers to bunch together into trough lines. Such airmass troughs must not be confused with cold fronts, which they resemble. The air behind an airmass trough is the same as that ahead whereas with a cold front the air behind the front will be colder and more unstable than the air ahead. Further the showers from a trough will often only last for an hour or less to be followed by a long clear interval.

There is a lot to commend the idea that a Polar airmass has only a certain potential to produce showers. If it uses up its energy in forming many showers along a trough line it has to 'rest' for a while both before and after. So often a long period which is clear of showers, when showers were forecast, is the harbinger of a nasty, sometimes squally, trough upwind just gathering its strength to bear down on you later.

The diagram of a model depression indicates that when the cold front clears the depression should also be passing, but that is not always so.

Depressions, whose centres slow up to the north of the observer, will continue to push their fronts on in their circulation and eventually there will be fronts moving into other parts of the pressure pattern which have little or no connection with their mother depression. This is how disembodied fronts are to be found on most weather charts and they are the ones which produce sometimes unforecast deteriorations. Just because it would appear you are in the circulation of an anticyclone does not mean that some old front cannot produce rain or drizzle and cut down the visibility considerably. It is in the middle of highs and ridges of high pressure that fronts will have least chance of producing anything nasty but, as pointed out elsewhere, the clouds of such fronts are rubbed out slowly from the top downwards and that process often leaves a total cover of low cloud. As you cannot see you have no means of knowing that up above the stratocumulus layer that is raining or drizzling on you it is clear as a bell. This layer of thick Sc cloud is often all that is left of kata fronts – those that are being eroded by air sinking above them. To help assess the situation, stratocumulus is a cloud of benign situations so you need not expect anything very dire from the persistence of this cloud along the line of an old front. Recognition that you have an old front passing can help passage-making as it indicates a veer of wind to come which may help to lay a new beating course you might otherwise not have been able to approach.

39 Occlusions

Once a depression begins to occlude it is past its prime and is in the process of filling up. The cold front that overtakes the warm front (see figure 39.1a) where the airmass behind the cold front is colder than that ahead of the warm front produces a cold occlusion while figure 39.1b shows the warm occlusion process. In both cases the effect is to gradually remove the warm sector phase of the weather of a depression and cut off the warm airmass aloft. Thus the warm front characteristics of cloud and rain are in evidence ahead of an occlusion, but when the occlusion passes at the surface the weather changes without a substantial break to cold front weather with possibly heavy showers mixed with more continuous rain. There should be a veer of wind and the barometer should rise. However as occlusions usually do not produce a very sharp fall in pressure the rise is correspondingly muted. Many fronts that cross Britain and the Continent

Schematic cross-section through (a) a cold occlusion where the air behind is colder than ahead and (b) a warm occlusion where the air behind is not as cold as that ahead.

figure 39.1a

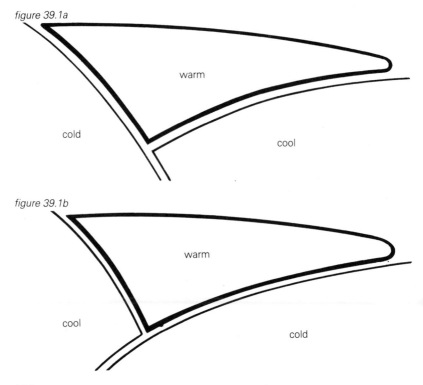

figure 39.1b

are occlusions and the further from the Atlantic you move the more likely is it that fronts which pass will be occlusions.

40 The message in cirrus

The problem with being alone on the ocean and looking at the weather is that you can only see the weather you have. Thus for wider coverage you have to rely on the forecasts or actual reports that go with them. The importance of knowing the basic models of met is that they help you read more into the forecasts and make inferences beyond present conditions. For example the steady encroachment of cirrus clouds from the west or northwest is not important in itself. What is important is what the sight of cirrus says about the coming conditions.

Because cirrus forms so high in the thin end of the wedge of warm air that is the warm front (or occlusion), and the other, thick end of the wedge, is embedded deeper in the depression (where conditions of wind and seaway are worse) so cirrus gives warning of those conditions. But let's try to be more accurate.

Not all cirrus is the same and its forms are almost infinitely varied. However there are features of these high ice-crystal clouds you should learn to recognize. The first thing to realize is that a cirrus cloud is an ice shower in the high atmosphere. The hooked appearance of cirrus elements, that have long been recognized as forming a 'windy sky', is due to the tails of the hooks (which are in fact showers of ice crystals) falling into slower air immediately below the heads of the hooks. We now know that this is a way of recognizing the otherwise invisible jet stream. If you look at figure 40.1 you will see that in a typical example, taken from the summer season (it is often stronger in winter), the heads of the cirrus clouds are moving on at some 90 knots, but not far below the wind speed has dropped to some 60 knots. Thus the tails are left behind by the galloping heads. The stronger the change in wind speed with height (what is called wind shear) the more strongly angled will be the hooks.

Thus when you first see cirrus forming look at its shape. Is it strongly hooked? If it is, contemplate trouble to come, but make more observations. Is the cirrus travelling fast? The rule of thumb here is that if you can see the cirrus actually moving against the backdrop of the sky, even from the unstable platform of a yacht, then its speed is upward of 80 knots and that means jet speed.

Having decided that a jet is associated with the cirrus remember, from the foregoing, that young, vigorous, developing depressions form to the

figure 40.1

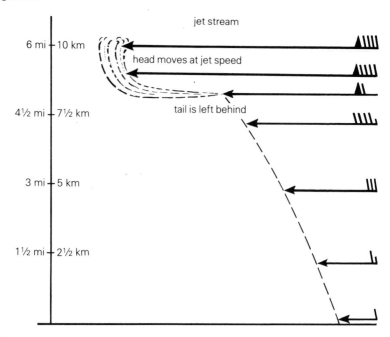

How a cirrus cloud gains its characteristic shape.

south of the jet. Thus fast-moving cirrus from NW or W usually means that a low is developing to the southwest and will run up to lambast you later.

However not all jets induce the most virulent depressions – those that will produce severe gales or even storm-force winds. You can get an idea if the coming low is to produce very strong wind at the surfaces if:

i the cirrus moves very fast showing a stronger than normal jet
ii the cirrus fallstreaks combine together to create great banners across the sky (see photograph 11). You are near to being under the jet when the northern sky is almost entirely clear of cloud and the northern edge of the cirrus banners is clean-cut as if it had been pared off with a knife

The form of the cirrus described above is different from any other form. For one thing it is denser and seems to come lower in the sky than other forms. However a long experience has proved to me on many occasions that the sight of such cirrus banners stretched, often NW to SE, across the sky is followed by a Force 9–10 somewhere not too far away. Even if that somewhere is not exactly in your sea area it will still raise the wind there to uncomfortable and even dangerous proportions.

So learn to recognize cirrus and its motion that foretells gales and for the few, but very important, occasions when it is really going to be a corker of a blow remember the form of jet cirrus.

On other occasions cirrus may not form in lines whose major features all point one way. The fallstreaks may point in two or more directions (see photograph 12). In that case the winds at closely spaced levels are in widely different directions and the nearer these directions are to being at right angles to one another the more they indicate very little wind aloft and therefore no nasty lows being born out to the west. This follows because there is obviously no jetstream with such low speed and contrary winds. At other times cirrus may form in lines, but you cannot see it move. That also means that any deterioration the cirrus heralds will not be a bad one. If you see long fallstreaks flowing right down the sky from quite dense heads then expect thunderstorms (if they are possible or likely) but even if no storms develop any rain or showers to follow will often be heavy.

41 The great temperature tie-up

Airmasses, jetstreams, lows and fronts can all be tied together in a vast three-dimensional structure with some simple modern ideas about how the winds blow aloft.

Surface winds, as we know, *blow to keep Low Pressure on their Left; Upper winds*, on the other hand, *blow to keep Low Temperature on their Left*. We have already seen how the jetstreams are irrevocably linked to the formation of depressions. In figure 41.1 typical upper wind contours (fine lines) are drawn over surface isobars (thick lines) for a simple model depression.

We see that the upper winds bend round the warm airmass to keep low temperature air on their left and the warm air on their right. The level of the upper winds is about the height that most cirrus clouds form so the mariner can detect the wind direction and get an idea of its speed from the movement of cirrus riding in that wind. It is worth emphasizing that the atmosphere *has* to work this way. There are no other possibilities than that the high speed upper winds must blow to keep low temperature on their left and so must curve round the model low as shown. However it is also imperative that the surface winds blow to keep low pressure on their left and a glance at A in figure 41.1 shows at once that there has also to be a certain irrevocable relationship between the directions of the wind blowing along the surface isobars and that blowing along the upper contours.

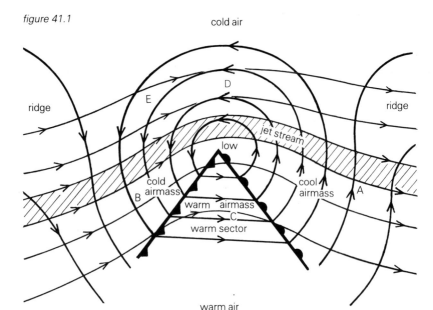

Upper winds over surface winds of a developed (but still developing) depression.

The wind that blows along the isobars is somewhat different from that which blows across the sailing yacht. The wind at isobar height is assumed to be that at 2000 ft up and it is usually stronger and is veered somewhat to the surface wind. We are going to call the 'isobar' wind the *gradient* wind – or sometimes, in this context, the lower wind L, to differentiate it from the wind at cirrus height which will be the upper wind U.

A yacht at A in figure 41.2 is well ahead of the coming warm front of the depression and has cirrus coming down from about WNW at high speed. The gradient wind is from SSW and you will note that the two winds are blowing at right angles across one another to obey the rule *Stand back to the lower wind and if the upper wind comes from the left hand a warmer airmass is approaching from a direction roughly half way between the two wind directions.*

If at A you already have, what you judge to be, a Polar airstream (it is relatively clear and grows heap clouds) then if a warmer airmass is on the way there must be a warm front to come. But a warm front also signifies a depression to come and all the wind, rain and squalls that that usually entails. The shape and motion of the cirrus can tell in some measure whether the depression will be vigorous or not. In the case shown it will be vigorous as its centre is south of the jet and it must therefore be developing.

figure 41.2

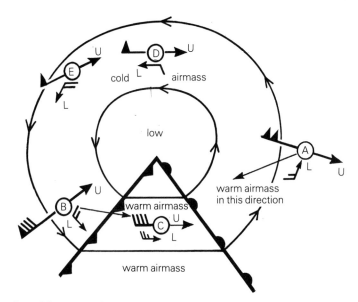

The situation of fig 41.1 reduced to speeds and directions of winds at cirrus levels (U) and at cumulus levels(L). This illustrates the basis of the 'crossed winds' rules.

Now look at B. A yacht there is just breaking into clearing skies as the cold front moves away. It has been rough and there is hope for better weather now. What are the chances?

In the model low shown there is a ridge of high pressure to come as the low moves on. But how do *you* know that? Could there not equally be a nasty, more vicious, secondary poised somewhere out to the west just waiting to speed in and deteriorate the weather?

Let us look at the wind orientations at B when a ridge is to come. You will see that the gradient wind (lower wind) is from about NW behind the cold front while the upper wind is from SW. These two winds are crossed to one another in the opposite sense to A and obey the rule *Stand back to the lower wind and if the upper wind comes from the right hand a colder airmass is coming in.*

It is a fact that the air over most anticyclones is colder than normal, whatever it may feel like on the ground, so this orientation will say that the weather is to improve, for a while at least. If there were another secondary to come it would have to form to the south of the jetstream and so the winds aloft at a position like B could not stream from the SW. The jet would have to be held back to the north and the winds aloft remain with a much more westerly or northwesterly tendency which would not fit the rule half as well.

So when a cold front clears look at the way the cirrus clouds along its receding trailing edge move, and compare this to the direction of the gradient wind. You can tell what the latter is from the movement of cumulus or other low cloud you will almost certainly have. If not see page 158 to obtain the gradient direction from the surface direction. If the winds are crossed as above expect improvement, even if it takes a while and a great many squally showers before it does so. However if the gradient and upper winds are far more parallel look out, or listen out, for the next depression on its way.

Incidentally if the showers you expect to follow the passage of a cold front do not materialize, or are very short-lived and soon die away, this is another sign that the next depression is on its way. When the cold airmass sweeps down from northern seas to prepare the ground for a substantial ridge of high pressure there must be shower clouds or at least big cauliflower cumulus coming along for a day or two. If showers quickly die out look for trouble.

The fact that A is ahead of the worst of the low that is to come and B is ahead of eventual improvement means that we can re-phrase the crossed winds rules thus:

Crossed winds rule for worsening weather – Stand back to the gradient wind and if high clouds advance from the left hand the weather will usually deteriorate.

Crossed winds rule for improving weather – Stand back to the gradient wind and if high clouds advance from the right hand the weather will usually improve for several days. (Mnemonic: Low weather follows when high clouds come from the Left hand.)

Although these rules have been culled from consideration of a model of a depression I have found through much practice that they work on many other situations that are not so obviously connected with a developing low. For example there are nearly always crossed winds for worsening weather when old fronts swim into a set-fair picture. The crossing angle will not be so obviously close to 90° as it is with the full-blooded fronts of new depressions but it will be there.

Sometimes what looks like jet cirrus comes in from odd directions. It often was jet cirrus once, but has now lost touch with the jet, or the jet has lost momentum and died leaving the cloud to fend for itself. In these cases the crossed winds rules help a great deal because they will usually indicate at once that the orientation of the high cloud to the lower wind is almost parallel.

This latter orientation provides the third useful crossed winds rule: *Crossed winds rule for little change* – If upper and lower winds are travelling parallel (or antiparallel) then the situation will not change for a while.

In figure 41.2 you will see that in the warm sector at C any cirrus to be seen will be travelling in the same direction as the low clouds. The next major change will be when the cold front comes along and that may be some time yet. Before the cold front actually arrives the upper and lower wind directions will begin to diverge.

When you are closely to the north of a depression centre you often cannot see the high sky, but when you can you will find that the wisps of cirrus will be moving more-or-less exactly against the direction that low clouds are moving. As long as that orientation continues there will not be a great deal of change. Later a yacht originally on position D will begin to feel the effects of the cold NE or N winds and then its position with respect to the depression will be as at E when the 'crossing for improvement' orientation is beginning to open up. As the depression is on its way out and the jet is to the south, improvement is going to come.

In this and many other ways the crossed winds rules can be used to help supplement the forecasts with your own observations. I can vouch for the fact that they work as since I left the professional meteorological service I have used them continuously to monitor coming weather changes and have rarely found them wanting.

You may ask, 'What about clouds riding in winds below low and high? Do they obey the rules too?' The answer to that is that they do sometimes and one of the most important times is when summer thunderstorms are involved. A particular situation of importance, because of the number of craft involved and the time of year, is the thundery incursions that breed over France and move up across the Channel in summer. The wind is invariably from some point east when these nasty brutes advance from the south spitting lightning, rolling thunder and often inducing squalls of dangerous proportions along their lines of advance. One such on a summer Sunday afternoon some years ago was the cause of most of the many fleets of dinghies sailing off the coasts of Southeast England capsizing almost to a man as a prodigious gust of some 50–60 knots cascaded out of a squall-line associated with the thundery situation that moved up across the Channel soon after the afternoon racing had started. The morning had seen very poor visibility, as it often does ahead of these systems, with a light easterly. The sudden change to temporary storm force from such light beginnings is typical of thundery lows. They can be very nasty while they last. See pages 142–5 for the way the rules work in this situation.

Occasionally storms are not conventional ones, but are born and grow one to two miles up sprouting like mushrooms out of the bed of a warm front. The clouds that stream in ahead of the worst of the storm are ones like those in photograph 11. Because they resemble lines of battlements in one form or flocks of sheep in another they are called altocumulus castellanus and floccus respectively. These clouds are worth recognizing as harbingers of thunder. It may be they appear in the morning, disappear as the day gets very hot and then reappear in great thickening bands, or islands and, finally, sheets of dark and forbidding hue in the afternoon. They are clouds of the medium levels (as their name 'alto' suggests) and they obey the crossed winds rule for deterioration.

At other times, when the thundery conditions are destined for others and not for you, the crossed winds rule for no change is obeyed with the altocumulus flowing in parallel to the lower wind. It is my experience that when thunderstorms are in the offing it is not cirrus, but the alto clouds that move most nearly at right angles to the gradient wind and warn of a deteriorating and potentially dangerous situation.

Not every situation that may be resolved by use of the crossed winds rules can be treated here. You have to use them and then with experience you find how they work on various situations. Suffice to say that the rules, being based on how the atmosphere as a whole must act, are as applicable for Boston, Vancouver or Vladivostock as they are for Atlantic Europe. In fact throughout the temperate latitudes of either hemisphere the rules work. In the southern hemisphere you stand facing the wind rather than with your back to it, but the rest of the wording and effects apply. Where the rules will not work is in the Tropics and certainly not near the Equator. If you intend to cruise those kind of waters you must read up on Tropical meteorology – this book dwells on the temperate latitudes.

42 Recognizing coming depressions from the crossing of upper and lower winds

The diagrams that follow give some typical examples of how to locate and do some detective work on coming depressions.

a Depression travelling on a normal track
Forecast clues
  i Crossed winds foretell developing depression in direction indicated.
 ii Speed and density of cirrus give indication of severity.
iii Steady change of one cloud type to another ie cirrus to cirrostratus (haloes) and then to altostratus (watery sun) is pattern of most intense systems. Holes in the build-up indicate an older system.

figure 42.1

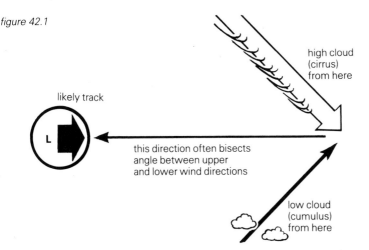

The normal way in which high and low clouds move when a depression is approaching.

b Depression travelling on some track other than the normal one from the Atlantic

Forecast clues

i Although crossed winds indicate a developing low, note speed of cirrus. It may not be moving very fast nor be very dense indicating a less vigorous system than previous example.

ii Look for either a steady or intermittent build-up of clouds to tell if system is likely to be more or less vigorous.

When a depression is on an unusual track.

figure 42.2

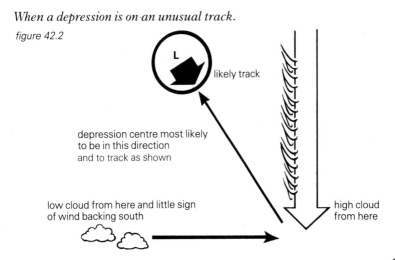

figure 42.3

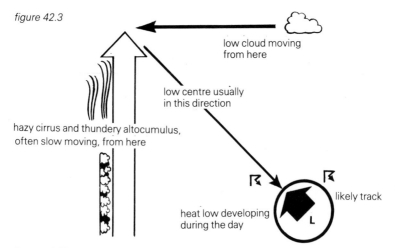

low cloud moving
from here

low centre usually
in this direction

hazy cirrus and thundery altocumulus,
often slow moving, from here

likely track

heat low developing
during the day

Potentially thundery situation with an easterly surface wind.

c Depression forming or moving from southerly point (typical heat-low system in English Channel area)

Forecast clues

   i Winds crossed for deterioration, but upper cloud slow moving. Upper sky often hazy.
  ii Easterly surface wind sometimes; poor visibility.
 iii As before likely track bisects angle between the crossed winds.
  iv Can use movement of high altocumulus (chaotic sky) to presage thunder (photograph 9).

High and low clouds in much the same direction signify a non-changing situation – although not necessarily good weather.

figure 42.4

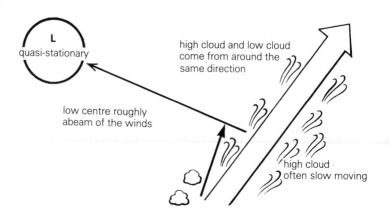

L
quasi-stationary

high cloud and low cloud
come from around the
same direction

low centre roughly
abeam of the winds

high cloud
often slow moving

d Depression slow moving

Forecast clues

i History of mainly cyclonic weather ie cloudy and periods of rain.

ii Parallel winds show little change.

iii Upper cloud should not be moving fast. If it is, monitor situation via forecasts to see if better or worse weather is coming.

43 Following the progress of a real depression

Depressions often do not act exactly as the textbooks say. The virtue in knowing the normal sequence of events lies in being able to notice when things are not going as they should.

If, for example, on yesterday's TV weather forecast there was a low lined up west of Ireland and it was forecast to move across the North Midlands of England en route for the North Sea with the associated fronts swinging in across the land and sea areas to the south. Rain from those fronts was forecast, but how have things gone today?

Rain came through during the night from a disembodied front that had lost touch with any depression centre. There are many such fronts and sometimes they can produce a considerable amount of rain although it is rare for them to be associated with strong blows. In this case the arrival of the rain and its passage during the hours of darkness, just as forecast, gives confidence that everything that follows will also go the same way. However that is sometimes a wrong assumption. Do not relax your vigilance; as the day gathers scan the high sky for the cirrus that ought to show if the coming depression is on schedule both timewise and by position.

Assume you are somewhere in mid-Channel (the exact position is not very important) and around 0800–0900 you are almost relieved to see the cirrus bands streaming in from a little north of west. That is what should be happening, but is everything else correct? Is the wind backing south? No it is not! And it does not do so all the morning even though the sun sports a halo as the cirrus changes to cirrostratus.

As the winds are not significantly crossed there is little sign of development in the coming depression. So you need not expect much danger from this low – yet. It took about three hours for the cirrus to change to cirrostratus so you might expect the next significant change – to altostratus with loss of the sun – to come along a similar length of time later still. That puts it around 1400–1500 before there is cloud thick enough to produce rain and this would also be the earliest time when the wind would increase markedly if it were going to do so.

So having made a forecast of when any real trouble might ensue you can watch to see what happens. It turns out to be a warm morning with the hazy sun occasionally breaking more brightly through holes that constantly appear and disappear. Such coming and going of the sun in the build-up to a front is another sign that this is not a full-blooded developing system. Suspect that it is an occluding front and therefore expect no warm sector and so little risk of sea fog.

The early afternoon sees no real change in the wind direction and the sun still manages to shine wanly through the white vault above. So what is the depression doing? It is probably going to produce something over your area eventually, otherwise there would have been no cirrus this morning and no thickening into halo cloud as has occurred.

So you wait and then suddenly things change. The wind rapidly alters direction to come in from the south and the sun just as quickly disappears. It is late afternoon before the rain comes, but there is little wind increase. It just rains rather persistently and very damply for hour after hour while the wind grows a force or so during the night. Next morning it is still raining, but the wind has gone round to the northwest in a series of shifts often accompanied by a change in the pattern of the rain. So we are not surprised to find that the general synopsis tells us that the depression has chosen to track through just to the north of us rather than going through much further north as first forecast.

We have experienced what the shipping forecasts describe as 'cyclonic' wind shifts (see next section) and have been given the benefit of the full period of rain that exists close to depression centres. The other possibility to have watched for is that the centre had tracked south. The basic criterion for that possibility would have been a wind that backed east and stayed that way for a long period before eventually backing still further into the northern quadrants as the centre cleared away eastwards. (See Cyclonic winds and weather.)

What can be expected now if the sky does not clear? Probably troughs with rain, showers and/or drizzle as these tend to gyrate round low centres like the spokes of a wheel. The darkening of the windward horizon often tells that such a trough is imminent. It may, for all you know, be the final clearing trough, but you can only tell when the skies break and big cumulus clouds develop in the aftermath.

Obviously example after example of the weather not running quite as forecast could be cited. However enough has been said to indicate the way you should imbibe the substance of the forecast and then monitor what the real weather does.

146

44 Cyclonic winds and weather

The term 'cyclonic' is used in two different contexts. When used in shipping or other forecasts it means that the forecasters cannot possibly describe the many changes of direction of the wind that will accompany the passage of a low through the area. They therefore leave it to the mariner to watch his wind direction and the sky so that he can make up his own mind as to whether the centre will track to the south, to the north or straight over him. In each case there will be rules which you should try to follow.

Typical cyclonic wind and weather changes

Position with respect to the low centre	(A)	(B)	(C)
Wind at first	E–SE and of some strength	Between S and E and of some strength	S–SE possibly fresh or strong
Weather at first	Clouding over if not already overcast. Visibility usually good; occasionally poor	Cloudy or overcast, some rain possible. Visibility normally good	Cloud and rain increasing as is normal with a warm front or occlusion approaching
Wind later	Backing E–NE and falling lighter	Light variable and possibly calm for a time in the eye of the low. Very near centre expect odd shifts that do not obey Buys Ballot's Law (page 159)	Veering SW–S

Weather later	Periods of rain or drizzle. Misty but rarely foggy	Often very low cloud with fairly continuous rain or drizzle	Clearance to warm sector kind of weather. Risk of fog patches
Wind finally	Backing N–NW and picking up in speed	Picking up from a westerly point. Possibly increasing strong or even gale	Veering W–NW with passage of a cold front – perhaps squalls
Weather finally	Rain, drizzle and low cloud slow to clear. Visibility may remain poor for a considerable time	Slow clearance of low cloud and rain. Periods of poorer weather on troughs swinging round main centre	Clearance to cooler, clearer conditions typical of Polar airstream. End of any fog risk

Cyclonic and anticyclonic isobars

The word cyclonic is also used to describe the curvature of isobars on a weather map.

Because of the way in which the atmosphere works it is always the case that:

i where isobars bend in the sense of enclosing lower pressure the air there must by its nature be generally rising. This sense of curvature is called cyclonic C

ii where isobars bend in the reverse sense ie to enclose high pressure, the air there must generally be sinking. This sense of curvature is called anticyclonic A

Rising air leads to more cloud, more precipitation, both continuous and showery, and poorer weather conditions generally while sinking air erodes clouds, makes precipitation less or prevents it altogether and in the case of showers inhibits them to such an extent that they become weak or non-existent.

Recognition of the sense of curvature of the isobars from a weather map gives an immediate idea of the likely conditions in that area. The forecast will go for certain weather conditions, but their severity will differ from area to area and so the degree of curvature be it cyclonic or anticyclonic will help you to make up your mind about the trend of conditions.

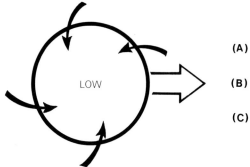

figure 44.1

(A)

(B)

(C)

Cyclonic winds and weather.

Of course isobars shift as the weather they inscribe shifts, but even the short glimpse of the Atlantic weather chart on TV can be some help if the sense of the isobaric curvature over an area of interest is noted in the short time available. The curvature is cyclonic wherever the isobars bend as if to enclose low pressure however far away that low may be.

Areas of cyclonic (C) and anticyclonic (A) curvature on a typical weather map.

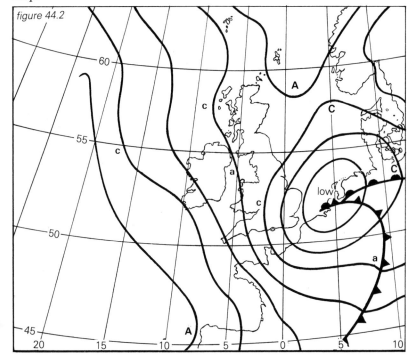

figure 44.2

If it appears that cyclonic curvature will exist over the area, or you have plotted a simple weather map using a shipping forecast and actuals that shows this trend, expect the conditions to be worse than, or as bad as, forecast. However the degree of curvature affects the severity of the cyclonic weather. In figure 44.2 capital letters show regions of sharp curvature and small letters regions of low curvature. Obviously along the warm front we must expect continuous rain and low cloud, but the isobars across the cold front do not show much curvature so it will be relatively weak. At points with capital A the curvature is strongly anticyclonic and most high clouds will disappear. This does not mean that low clouds will necessarily disappear, but generally there will be no precipitation in these areas. The small a's indicate weak anticyclonic curvature. Just behind the cold front the cloud could well break here for a time, but more cyclonic curvature is to follow so the break will be short lived.

Returning to a mnemonic used earlier we can say that *Veed isobars pointed towards higher pressure mean a Valley or (trough)*. This helps sort out cyclonic from anticyclonic curvature in regions where the sense of the curvature is not immediately obvious.

45 Measuring wind speed from a weather map

If isobars are drawn at intervals of 2 millibars apart the speed of the wind at about 2000 ft (600 m) can be assessed. Amongst other things this figure puts an approximate ceiling on the speed of the gusts that can occur. To measure the wind speed from the isobars a geostrophic wind scale is used. If the term geostrophic is unfamiliar and apparently complex do not be put off. The construction of a geostrophic scale is very easy and can be helpful.

The geostrophic wind blows along the isobars where they are more-or-less straight and results from a balance between an apparent force, called the geostrophic force F and the pressure gradient force P. Geostrophic force occurs because the air is moving on a rotating earth and the reasons for it are not important to the practical sailor who just wants to know what the result is. The pressure gradient force is easier to understand being the chosen pressure interval (2 mb in our case) divided by the distance apart D of the isobars (see figure 45.1).

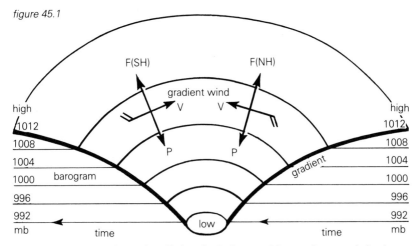

figure 45.1

An analogy method for visualizing the balance of forces that result in the gradient wind. The wind blows in opposite senses round the low centre in the two hemispheres.

The resultant geostrophic wind V blows between the opposing actions of these two forces and is related to them such that for a given scale of chart

distance apart of the isobars × geostrophic wind speed = constant

or

$$DV = \text{constant}$$

We see at once from this that if the distance apart of the isobars should halve, the corresponding wind speed must have doubled. So this simple relationship holds the key to the fact that *The wind speed increases as the isobar spacing becomes tighter.*

Most people know this simply from looking at weather maps on the TV,

How to construct a geostrophic wind scale.

figure 45.2

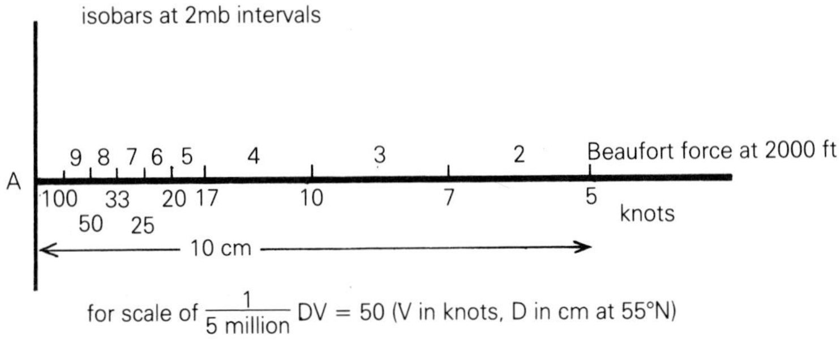

isobars at 2mb intervals

for scale of $\frac{1}{5 \text{ million}}$ DV = 50 (V in knots, D in cm at 55°N)

151

but to find out what the actual wind speed will be we can proceed as follows.

For a chart whose scale is 1 in 5 million we can construct the geostrophic wind scale simply from the fact that at 55°N and for isobars spaced 2 mb apart

$$DV = 50 \qquad \text{(D in cm, and V in knots)}$$

So we see straight away that if we take an origin line A (see figure 45.2) the mark for 5 knots must be 10 cm away, the mark for 20 knots is 2½ cm away and that for 50 knots is 1 cm away from A.

This is self evident in figure 45.2 and we can neglect changes in latitude when sailing between about 50°N and 60°N. Even in lower latitudes (down to 45°N) the error introduced by neglecting latitude is less than other errors that are inherent in using the geostrophic scale. So effectively we can forget latitude variation and use the scale in most of the temperate latitudes.

If your chart is a different scale the basic distances above are altered by multiplying by the ratio of 5 million to the corresponding scale figure of your chart. For example on a scale of 1 in 2.5 million the geostrophic scale expands by a factor of 2. If you have isobars at 4 mb intervals rather than 2 mb then again the scale expands by a factor of 2. So to construct a scale for a 1 in 5 million chart with isobars at 4 mb intervals use $DV = 100$ in making your scale.

For use at sea draw the scale on thin card and then encapsulate it in clear plastic, sealing the edges with clear sticky tape. Leave room at one end to punch a hole to take a length of cord that prevents the device getting lost. If you use two different kinds of weather chart blank put the other scale on the reverse side.

The geostrophic wind scale you have made will measure the wind speed at about 2000 ft providing the isobars are not too curved. When they become substantially curved there is also a considerable correction to be applied to the measured wind speed. The geostrophic speed with the correction is called the 'gradient wind speed'.

The ideas of cyclonic and anticyclonic curvature have already been discussed in Section 44. Although there is a continuous correction to be applied, depending on how curved the isobars are, it is unlikely that the practical yachtsman will ever wish to be so precise in his measurements as to want to use the exact figures. So we will provide some rules of thumb which will give a figure as close as necessary to the correct speed. The rule is *The true gradient wind speed G becomes less than the measured geostrophic V as the isobars become more cyclonically curved.* The factor by which to modify V to obtain a figure closer to the true gradient speed can be assessed from figure 45.3. For example if close to the low centre, where the isobars are very strongly curved, we lay the geostrophic scale across the isobars and find the speed is 60 knots do not be too alarmed.

152

figure 45.3

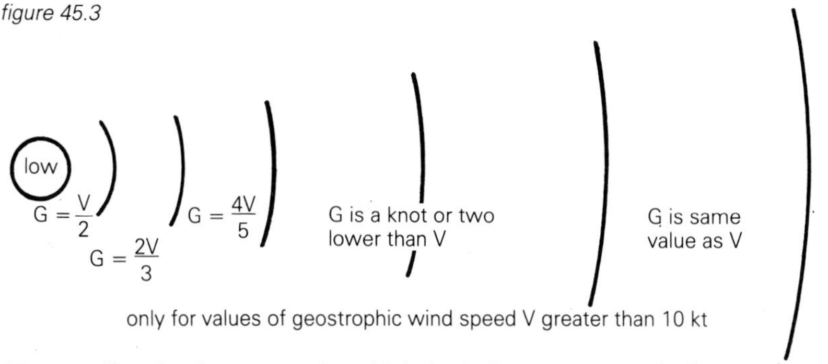

$$G = \frac{V}{2}$$

$$G = \frac{2V}{3}$$

$$G = \frac{4V}{5}$$

G is a knot or two lower than V

G is same value as V

only for values of geostrophic wind speed V greater than 10 kt

How to allow for the amount by which the isobars are curved when assessing the gradient wind using a geostrophic scale.

Halve it to find the likely true gradient speed ie 30 knots (it will be less than this anyway as our approximate method overestimates the gradient speed) and then reduce that figure again by a third to find the likely surface wind speed. You then obtain a manageable 20 knots surface wind speed, but with a potential to produce 30 knot gusts at times. Certainly here, close to the low there will not be anything like the horrific 60 knots falsely measured by the geostrophic scale. As you go further out the gradient values become closer and closer to the measured geostrophic ones.

The curvature of isobars that bend in an anticyclonic way is too small to make it worth offering any advice about corrections. Use the geostrophic scale and call the wind you find the 'gradient wind'.

To tie up the ideas with a model, figure 45.1 shows a barogram as a low centre tracks through an area. The funnel shape of the barometer changes leads to a gravitational analogy where the air would slip down the gradient under the gradient force P, but is prevented from doing so by the geostrophic force F. The situation in the temperate latitudes of both hemispheres is shown, on the left for the southern (SH) and on the right for the northern (NH). Because the isobars are curved the actual wind blowing along the isobars is the gradient wind (which we now know how to find). We see how the isobars become more tightly spaced as the gradient increases, but we must also remember that the gradient wind factor comes into play when the isobars become more curved.

Assessing the surface wind speed

With the knowledge of the gradient wind speed (G) the surface speed can be assumed to be

a two thirds of G over the sea
b a third of G over the land

figure 45.4

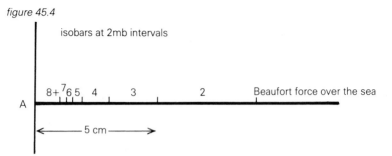

Geostrophic scale to measure wind speed over the sea directly.

So from a measured gradient speed of 25 knots we would expect the mean wind speed over the sea to be about 16 knots and over the land less than 10 knots. Figure 45.4 is a geostrophic scale modified to read Beaufort force directly from the isobar spacing.

These are average values, however, and there are other rules that will help modify the above rules of thumb and make an educated guess into a nearer certainty.

Over land – By day the surface wind climbs to a value closer to G in the middle of the afternoon and then falls with evening. By night the surface wind can fall as low as half G.

Typical values of wind speed over the land and over the sea during a 24 hour period compared to the measured gradient wind speed.

figure 45.5

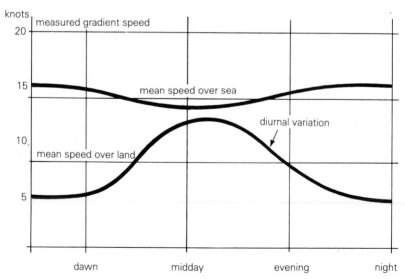

Over the sea – The variations in speed are much less marked, but the maximum wind speed may occur in the early hours of the morning.
In both cases:
By day – The wind speed becomes closer to G when skies are clear (or populated with cumulus clouds) than when it is overcast.
By night – There will be very little variation over the sea, but over land the wind speed will be lower when skies are clear than when it is cloudy.

In the above remember that off a windward coast the wind will have land characteristics and there will be some hints of these characteristics even when the nearest land upwind is 100 miles away.

Gusts can be up to gradient speed which may occasionally double the average surface wind speed. Expect the gusts to be strongest at the head of any heavy showers and to go above gradient speed sometimes, especially in thunderstorms.

The relationship between the various wind speeds is summed up in figure 11.2 (see page 52).

Moving the fronts on
Another use of the geostrophic scale lies in assessing how far a front on a weather map will have moved in the outlook period. It is based on the facts

How to use a geostrophic scale to move fronts on.

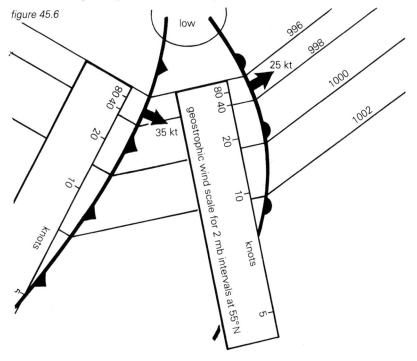

figure 45.6

155

that cold fronts and occlusions move with the speed of the wind behind them while warm fronts move at two thirds of the wind speed behind them. Thus if, as in figure 45.6, the scale is laid across the isobars behind a warm front and the average wind speed found, then assume the front moves at two thirds of the speed for the number of hours ahead you wish.

In the case considered the measured speed is just below 40 knots and, allowing for all the inherent errors, the front is moved on at 25 knots for say six hours making a total travel of 150 nautical miles. Similarly the cold front is found to move at about 35 knots and so covers over 200 miles in the same time. When there is doubt about the shape of the final front because the speeds measured at different points behind it are different, compromise and keep the average artistic form of curve rather than allow it to take up some impossible shape. In any case are you so sure your isobars are right? The method may not work sometimes, but in lieu of any other information it is the only method you have of finding the likely future positions and it will often show up the occlusion process taking place as cold fronts overtake warm ones so that what was a warm sector disappears before it reaches you.

46 Assessing the surface wind direction

The isobars show the direction of the gradient wind and it can be taken that when you see a weather map the surface wind will be from roughly the direction of the isobars. However the surface wind will:

a be angled in across the isobars at about 15° towards lower pressure over the sea

b be angled in at double this angle (about 30°) over the land

Wind over the coast
On leaving the land for the sea (windward coast) the wind speed increases and the direction comes closer to that of the isobars. On forsaking the sea for the land (leeward coast) the wind speed must decrease and the wind direction has to become more angled to the isobars.

What happens to the wind because of these effects is shown in figures 46.1 a and b for off-shore and on-shore winds. Winds closer to the lie of the coastline than the ones depicted will tend to be steered more-or-less along the coast and may well pick up in speed. This happened in the great Channel Race gale of August 1956 when the winds to the south of the low

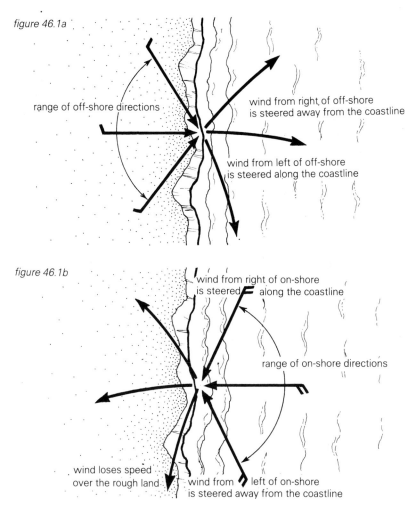

figure 46.1a

range of off-shore directions

wind from right of off-shore
is steered away from the coastline

wind from left of off-shore
is steered along the coastline

figure 46.1b

wind from right of on-shore
is steered along the coastline

range of on-shore directions

wind loses speed
over the rough land

wind from left of on-shore
is steered away from the coastline

*a) The way the wind direction changes off the coast when winds are
from the land. The reverse happens when the wind leaves the sea for
the land (b).*

centre (that came in over the Bristol Channel area) became storm force in
a corridor that swept the Solent area. It seems likely that some of that
ferocity was enhanced by this 'coast' effect.

On many days of summer, when the wind speed is 15 knots or more and
the wind is blowing at an angle not far off that of the coastline itself the
seabreeze effect puts a shorewards component on to the existing wind
close to the coast. More about this is to be found under Seabreeze effects
when the wind blows stronger (see page 175).

47 What's wrong with the wind?

The best guide to the direction of the gradient wind when you have no current weather map is to watch the direction of flight of low clouds such as cumulus (see photograph 8).

There are times when cumulus (or other low cloud) is seen to be moving in a widely different direction from the surface wind. The angle between the two winds becomes much greater than the 45° or so that is the most by which they might be expected to differ.

The reason may be one of the following:

i The surface wind is seabreeze. This can often be checked because the breeze will be blowing in an on-shore direction.

ii The surface wind is due to a local storm centre. Thunderstorms and big shower clouds can draw in their own local wind.

iii You are very close to an active front. In this case odd movements are often visible in the clouds above or coming.

iv The surface wind is due to the early formation of a small centre of low pressure nearby. Because air has mass and speed it has considerable momentum and takes time to become deflected from its original course at the behest of the production of a local centre of low pressure. The surface wind will be drawn towards the new low first while the air above continues to flow in its old direction.

How to assess the direction of the isobars or the direction of low pressure when beating.

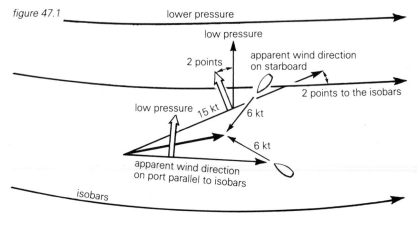

figure 47.1

lower pressure

low pressure

2 points

apparent wind direction on starboard

2 points to the isobars

low pressure 15 kt 6 kt

6 kt

apparent wind direction on port parallel to isobars

isobars

higher pressure

Which of these possibilities is the most likely will follow from the recent past history of the weather and what is happening right now.

Finding the isobar direction on land

The law which was given to the world early in the development of meteorology by Professor Buys Ballot of Utrecht and called 'Buys Ballot's Law' seems today, with our modern knowledge, very close to a cliché. However it is still as true and useful as it ever was.

Buys Ballot's Law is *Stand back to the wind and pressure is Low on your Left*; stated thus it applies to the northern hemisphere, but if you stand 'facing' the wind it is then correct for the southern hemisphere. The mnemonic of Low and Left should be noted.

Winds over the land are usually substantially different from the gradient wind. The gradient wind is the one which follows the line of the isobars and its height is taken to be that of the wind at 2000 ft.

The surface wind is always trying to blow out of high pressure into low and so is normally backed (shifted anticlockwise) to the gradient wind. The angle between the surface and gradient winds is often quite large eg 35–45°. So to find the direction of the gradient wind:

i stand back to the surface wind and then rotate through about 30–40° to the right ie clockwise. You will then be roughly looking along the isobars. At the same time low pressure is in the direction of your outstretched left arm or

ii note the direction of flight of low clouds like cumulus or broken stratus as these clouds ride in the gradient wind

Finding the direction of low pressure when beating

Because of the apparent wind it is not a simple task to find the surface wind, let alone the gradient wind. The lower pressure is normally found by standing back to the surface wind and then it is on the left hand. However it is really the gradient wind to which you should have your back and that is veered some 15–20° from the sea-surface wind.

To sort this out look at figure 47.1. The surface wind is the black solid arrow and is drawn 15° to the direction of the gradient wind. It is assumed your yacht makes about 6 knots when beating in this wind. Other wind speeds and boat speeds will make very little difference to the argument.

The vector triangle that gives the apparent wind shows that:

i on port tack the low pressure is abeam of the apparent wind, or put another way the isobars are in the direction of the apparent wind

ii on starboard tack the low pressure is two points abaft the beam of the apparent wind, or the isobars are two points to the right of the apparent wind direction

In either case, whether you have instruments or rely on a masthead flag or vane, it is the apparent wind you will be reading and thus, while the starboard tack rule is more complicated than the port tack rule, the rules will save a good deal of vector triangle drawing. For displacement sailing craft the rule will be right for most wind speeds.

48 How long before it blows?

This is always amongst the most difficult and yet most important questions. A forecast that is for the next 12 or 24 hours and goes for wind increasing sometime during the period is almost worse than no forecast at all, because you are then left in doubt as to exactly when the wind and sea will grow to, for you, unmanageable proportions.

Once you have heard a shipping forecast you are on your own for another six hours and land area forecasts are not going to help much. Their interest in wind is for the land or the immediate coastal strip of water and not for the deeper waters you may be sailing. A further complication is that any gale warnings given by coast radio stations in whatever country will, in general, be for Force 8 gales. As Force 6 is a 'yacht gale', the British local radio stations with their Small Craft Warnings already referred to in Section 5 and the Scandinavians, who also give warnings of Force 6 to 7 gales for their more sheltered Baltic waters from coast radio stations, stand alone in meeting the specific needs of yachts. Other countries still use the 'big ship' criterion of Force 8.

There are very few occasions when the wind will grow from 15 to 25 knots (Force 4 to 6) in an hour – not to provide sustained wind anyway. In general the wind increase in summer in the region of the English Channel is likely to be in a time span of less than 10 hours. If the wind speed does not grow to sizeable proportions in 10 hours and you are expecting the increase to come from an encroaching depression then either the depression has slowed up, moved in some other direction or is filling fast. In any of these cases there is plenty of time to make port remembering that there can always be another depression moving into the bed of cyclonic tendency created by the one which has not fully materialized. In which case the next blow could be the bad one.

Often with delayed blows there are indications in the clouds (page 144), or the wind, as it increases slowly, does not shift in direction as it should. It must be realized when giving advice about signs of increasing wind that the crew at sea can only see the wind rising and the barometer falling. What they cannot know is how fast the barometer will fall in the coming hours nor how much the wind will rise – or when.

However a survey I once did for the English Channel (see *Wind and Sailing Boats*, David and Charles 1973) showed that when the wind increase was due to encroaching depressions the shortest period for the wind to grow from a manageable Force 4 to a possibly potentially dangerous Force 6 was some three hours and the longest occupied a whole day. However in the summer months most of the increases occupied less than 10 hours and on average both for the year and just for the sailing season the rise time lay between 7 and 8 hours.

So while in other more stormy areas such as the exposed regions of the Atlantic-facing coasts (of Britain and France particularly) things might be somewhat different (with shorter rise times), where the majority of the pleasure sailing is done there is usually plenty of time not only to make a haven, but also to choose which haven. In this context because the deeper depressions tend to travel across Northern Britain and end up in Scandinavia so the increasing winds ahead of them come from the southern quadrants and yachts making shelter off coasts facing any direction other than north (of which there are relatively few) do so at good speed with the wind either behind them (not always the best) or on the beam. Such lucky attributes help to account for the very few fatal accidents to cruising yachts in deteriorating weather.

Having said all this, weather is such that you can never take anything for granted. Occasionally vicious summer blows appear in the English Channel where, for the most part, the weather is bland, but only the most unhappy set of circumstances will leave the mariner with no warning at all of such features. It is important all the time to listen to the forecasts, note carefully what they say and then keep your own watch on developments. In particular if dense jet cirrus starts rushing across your sky from about NW even before the barometer has showed much sign of falling start thinking about where you can get shelter not only from the sharp southerly blow it may portend, but also from the northwesterly that may follow the passage of a vortex that has developed and run along the powerbed of the warm, summer Channel. For example tucking yourself in along the north-facing coast of some island will be fine until the wind comes in behind the cold front and makes your sheltered haven a lee shore.

A great deal has been said above about the English Channel, but some location has to be given and the Channel has special attributes. Lows tend to follow it and develop as they come. Depressions set for Ireland and eventually the North Sea, change direction and move through it preferring the easy passage of the waterway to the fight over the high ground of western Britain. Having said which we expect somewhat similar attributes in the southern North Sea and generally more chance of trouble as we go further north. The Atlantic coasts of France are very exposed, but of course in summer the benign influence of the Azores anticyclone is more likely to affect them than latitudes further north.

Finally a word about barometers and their tendency. In forecasting wind the rate at which the barometer falls is nothing more than an immediate presage of trouble. It may fall, but when gales are to follow the rate of fall is often slow at first giving no early warning of coming danger. You may take any falling barometer as a warning and act accordingly, but experience shows that very often the fall is arrested long before the depth of the trough has become such as to tighten the local gradient into one associated with Force 6 let alone Force 8. So you need the sky signs and the wind signs to back up the barometer, plus of course the important intelligence of coming problems from the forecasts.

Criteria for gauging the strength of an imminent wind from barometric tendency are given on page 91, but this warning is of short duration and is of the kind that prompts the immediate bending on of heavy weather canvas, the closure of ventilators and the battening of hatches etc.

In conclusion do not forget the sign of the long low swell of which you may suddenly become aware in open waters moving from a direction where a storm is already in progress while your own wind and sea are of the slightest. The swell runs on fast as it is long and low and can warn of real trouble to come. Such a warning was well known to sailors of pre-satellite days who saw it as the first sign of very intense Atlantic depressions or, when in waters prone to them, of hurricanes. Today use the sign of the swell as a prompt to get a forecast.

How long before the rain?

For sailing there is nothing truly significant about rain, but consider the following points:

i rain and wind tend to come together

ii rain tends to beat down a seaway

iii in the build-up to the passage of warm fronts and occlusions the arrival of rain lowers the cloudbase, lowers morale, often indicates that stronger wind is imminent or brings it

iv normal rain does not appreciably lower visibility. In this it differs significantly from drizzle

v after a recent past history of encroaching frontal cloud the arrival of rain prompts thoughts as to what will inevitably follow. Normally there will be a warm front passing at some later time (see page 128) or an occlusion passing (see page 134)

vi if rain took a long time coming then the whole system may take equally long to pass

49 About highs

Because of their inherent danger a great deal has been said about depressions. However, much cruising time is spent under the influence of highs (anticyclones) so here are some useful facts about them.

Anticyclones are regions of sinking air. The air sinks from very high up and as it sinks it warms up by compression. This warming tends to make the higher clouds die out because they evaporate away. This usually makes the high sky under anticyclones fairly free of cloud; which does not mean that the air near the surface is also clear of cloud. Anticyclones can be very cloudy especially over the sea, but often, if the cloud is not too thick, the heat of the sun will lead to it disappearing also. Then the skies will become blue in the way that is popularly associated with highs.

The subsidence of air from aloft will produce, in anticyclones, what is called a subsidence inversion. The normal fall in temperature with height is overturned, or inverted, by the warmed layers above the ground and this kind of inversion is very strong and difficult for surface thermals to break. The other kind of inversion, the one that sets in over the land on most nights, is much more easily broken up by the sun's heat in the morning. Thus anticyclones gain their reputation for sluggish behaviour in general. If it is cloudy in an anticylone then expect the cloud to persist and if it is clear it is very likely that it will remain that way even in the heat of the day.

Anticyclones are of two kinds; those that travel and those that block. The latter persist more-or-less in the same place for days, weeks, or even, in some memorable years, for months.

Travelling highs are anticyclonic cells that are embedded in the circum-Polar westerlies and so form a kind of antidote to the travelling depressions. In most cases there will not be a whole anticyclone between one depression and another, only a ridge of high pressure from an anticyclone to the south somewhere. These highs do not interfere with the westerlies and the jetstream continues to blow around the zones of latitude it normally frequents. However when the blocking high interposes itself the jets are sent packing to climes north and south of the so-called 'block' and the depressions must go too. Blocking highs are sometimes responsible for the complete break-up of the usual weather patterns for months on end and when they stand invincibly over the Atlantic in summer the result is the heatwaves that Atlantic Europe experienced in such phenomenal years as 1959 and 1976. However, on the other hand, when they stick over Scandinavia in winter these shores are visited by the type of Arctic conditions usually reserved for latitudes much further north. Such a memorable one was 1963.

Undoubtedly the highs control the weather. If a blocking high intervenes, while those under its aegis experience good weather, places on its periphery are visited by unusually cyclonic weather. A blocking high over Britain often means bad weather for Spain and Southern Europe generally.

While the mariner can obtain some help with where the lows will develop he has no way of knowing where and when highs will develop. The computer can forecast the development of such features. Indeed its rather sluggish metabolism is well suited to working on large slow-moving features. Yet even it may not be able to see the odd set of circumstances that obtain when the whole atmosphere suddenly goes anticyclonic over thousands of square miles of ocean and land and a block of unusual intensity disrupts the global weather patterns.

50 On the edge of the high

The centres of anticyclones are clichés for fair weather. Yet on the edge of an anticyclone the pressure may be relatively high and steady, but the weather is not good. An old front may become trapped in the circulation and end up threading its way down the isobars rather than being across them. Then winds are often light and the clouds dense and variable. There are long periods of cloudiness with perhaps brief glimpses of the sun. It occasionally rains and drizzles. Then the light wind shifts from a direction that the weather chart showed was its correct direction and comes from some apparently impossible direction.

It may rain harder for a time and a little more wind comes along to make the passage slightly less frustrating. You look around the sky for signs of a break and later the cloudbase lifts, but will it rain any more? Look for a hard cloudbase with definite lumps that undulate below the base. From those areas rain, if it falls, will be of the lightest. There may be patches on the cloudbase which look fuzzy. From there the intermittent rain is falling and you can often detect these showery areas when you suddenly become aware that the lumps in the base have disappeared from view. Showers usually mean an increase in wind and gusts. These showers from highish cloud of an old front usually do not disturb the surface wind much, if at all. Except, and the exception is important, when fronts become thundery as they do when it is very warm for the time of year. Such fronts can occur throughout the sailing season and whether thundery or not the old front that sits and stays when all the met laws say it should be anticyclonic and sunny is bad for morale.

Periods of deterioration in these situations are usually due to waves

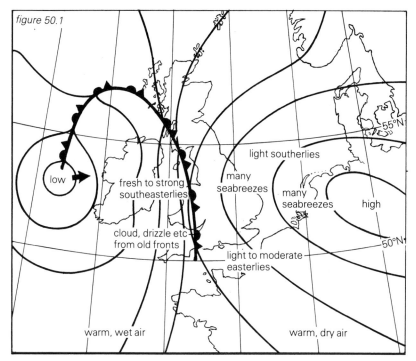

figure 50.1

low

fresh to strong southeasterlies

many seabreezes

light southerlies

many seabreezes

high

cloud, drizzle etc from old fronts

light to moderate easterlies

warm, wet air

warm, dry air

55°N

50°N

Strong winds over sea areas, a situation which occurs frequently. In this case the blow is in the Irish Sea when an encroaching low collides with an immobile high.

rippling down the front and this is why the wind often varies from one direction to another as temporary low pressure is built close by and then disappears again.

After that the skies may break and yet the wind remains light. Near the coast look out for the sudden generation of seabreezes when a cloudy forenoon gives way to sunshine in the afternoon. Sometimes, because the cloud is variable, it may remain wholly cloudy over the sea while over the land it has become temporarily sunny. This may suddenly generate a breeze almost against the expected wind direction. If it looks bright inshore or, better still, inland expect a breeze even though it is cloudy over the sea. The late spring and early summer days are the most energetic from the point of generating seabreezes whenever the conditions allow and when the breeze starts the resultant sinking air over the sea will nearly always clear the cloud there as well leaving other regions still predominantly cloudy.

When a high becomes established to the east and Atlantic lows begin to encroach to try and break it down the situation becomes one of relatively fair weather between the two systems, but winds can become strong or even gale. The idea of a low 'colliding' with the high as if a football were colliding with a rather flabby balloon is not a bad one and between the two the isobars often become very tight. The high is sometimes very loth to give way and the eventual change to cyclonic weather only comes after several days of transition from fair anticyclonic weather with light winds to overcast cyclonic weather with anything but light winds.

Thus the sight of HIGH on the chart over the landmass of Europe means a potentially dangerous situation exists over the Atlantic coasts and in the North Sea. The source of the airstream will then control the kind of weather that will ensue, but the wind needs-must have a southerly cant. If it comes from Biscay it will often be cloudy and showers or longer periods of rain are likely. If it comes from the direction of the Mediterranean it is most likely to be dry and relatively cloudless even if the wind does whip the spume off the tops of the waves.

This is occurring over the Irish Sea in figure 50.1.

51 About inversions

Inversions contribute a great deal to weather. The normal state of the atmosphere is to fall in temperature with height. It does so at quite definite rates which are called 'lapse rates'. There are two of these; the 'dry adiabatic lapse rate' (DALR) and the 'wet adiabatic lapse rate' (WALR). Any air parcel that rises or sinks and in which no cloud has formed changes temperature by about 5½°F for every 1000 ft of ascent or descent – the DALR. If it rises it cools and if it sinks it warms up. As soon as a rising parcel has fallen in temperature sufficiently for the water vapour in it to condense into cloud the action of condensing liberates latent heat

How subsidence (a) and overnight (b) inversions form.

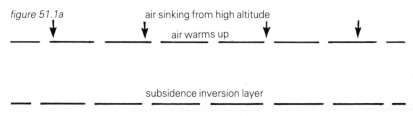

figure 51.1a   air sinking from high altitude

air warms up

subsidence inversion layer

cooler air below

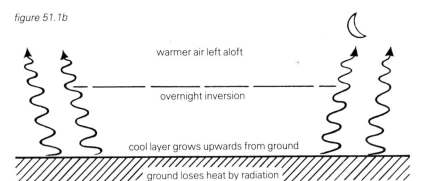

figure 51.1b

warmer air left aloft

overnight inversion

cool layer grows upwards from ground

ground loses heat by radiation

within the cloud and the rate at which the parcel cools now halves to a little over 2½°F per 1000 ft – the WALR.

Conversely when cloudy air sinks and warms up at the WALR it eventually gets warm enough to become 'dry' and so will now heat up at twice the rate it did before. Dry air that sinks in anticyclones is therefore in a position to get so warm near the surface that no amount of sunshine can create thermals that would punch holes in it. The weather is then cloud-free, very warm for the time of year and often very hazy. As the sun rises or sinks the blue top of the haze layer is often quite startlingly clear. Sight of such a phenomenon indicates better than anything that a strong subsidence inversion exists (see figure 51.1a).

The normal nighttime inversion comes into being by a quite different process. During the day turbulence and convection mix up the lowest layer of the atmosphere so that in the afternoon it is, for 2000 ft or more, all much the same temperature. In the evening, however, the earth and the air in contact with it cools. The turbulence does not reach up as high, for the wind sinks in speed and convection currents die away. Now the warm upper layer is cut off from contact with the cool surface layer and the normal situation of cooling progressively with height is up-ended or inverted. It is this situation which forms the inversion. From a sailing point of view the formation of the inversion at night is a land phenomenon, but as most nights are spent in close proximity to creek, estuary or marina so a great deal of cruising time is under its influence (see figure 51.1b).

For example the wind almost always suddenly drops in speed and shifts direction somewhat (usually backing) as the inversion forms. As it strengthens the wind progressively dies. Overnight stratocumulus cloud layers often form in inversions and these usually go just as readily when the sun attacks their tops during the morning. Sometimes however the cloud thickens especially when old or weak fronts are about and then the wind stays sluggish all day.

Even when the sun shines and it gets hot, seabreezes, which need convection currents to help them realize their full potential, will not readily form under inversions. So it is a fallacy that heat and breezes go hand in hand. In this connection it is only the subsidence inversion – and that means the influence of a strong anticyclone – that is tough enough to inhibit convection and so kill the seabreeze.

52 Heat seeks cold

The effect of an inversion layer is to inhibit change in the smallscale weather processes. The reason for this can be summed up in a simple universal law of nature which, while there are complicated ways of expressing it, can be simply stated as *Heat seeks cold*.

Let us take some examples, firstly the inversion. It is by definition warmer in an inversion layer than below. Thus the principle says that the heat in the inversion will try to seek the cooler air beneath. That means sluggish sinking currents which will inhibit the production of thermals that could speed things up. On the other hand when the surface is warmer than the air above – the normal situation of the atmosphere – heated parcels of air (thermals) take off to seek the higher, cooler realms and we have what is termed instability. The normal state of the atmosphere is to be, in part at least, unstable. The converse is, of course, stability which is the condition denoted by inversion layers.

If you think about it a warm front, whose surface may be many thousands of feet aloft, is an inversion layer and thus will produce stability in its vicinity. So why doesn't the warm air all sink through the frontal surface – that is what the principle of heat seeks cold suggests? The answer is in the diagrams of fronts to be found on pages 125–32. The zone of separation of the two air masses shown is not just to make the diagram easy to draw. There really is a layer of different air between the two surfaces that prevents them mixing and the practical result is that the warm air sits over the cold air and does not sink into it. However that does not prevent cool air below the frontal surface sinking and it is a matter of observation that the space below an encroaching ana warm front is usually as clear as a bell, all cloud there having been eroded away by sinking air and the inhibiting of convection currents. This is a useful attribute as it means that the warm fronts of the worst weather sweep their skies clean so that you can see the onset of cirrus and cirrostratus clouds that foretell the bad weather to come.

A cold front is also an inversion layer, but here the stability that goes with a warm front (or occlusion) is overcome by a much more vigorous

168

process of lifting as the cold air drives in like a wedge under the warm air above. This sets the warm air into an unstable state and the result is showers embedded, like cherries in a cake, mixed with the layer clouds (nimbostratus and altostratus) which are usually associated with warm fronts.

Such mechanical lifting of air layers is the same process that sets off showers over the foothills of mountain ranges when the wind is onshore and then the coastal plain is often clear. Mechanical lifting of this kind takes air that is already stable, and so would not seek higher levels of its own accord, to higher levels. It is often quite humid and the lifting cools it so that cold air exists over warmer air; this is the classic situation for the formation of showers.

The sea is the greatest reservoir of heat in the world. It communicates this heat to the air mainly through the medium of showers. Typical of the process are the vast fleets of shower clouds that grow in maritime Polar air in spring when it is drawn south behind depressions.

The sea isotherms increase rank upon rank below the cold humid mP air as it is drawn southwards making it more and more certain that thermal currents will lift off to seek the colder air aloft. Once a thermal source has started to generate a shower cloud it will tend to sweep the area around it clear of other clouds by the fact that while air is rising in the centre of the developing shower that around the periphery is sinking. Sinking air will erode cloud in the immediate environs of the developing shower so making for an individual cumulonimbus rather than what might otherwise be expected – a massive lifting of the whole airmass.

The biggest heat storms of all – thunderstorms – will take over a region about 15 miles square if they are moving very sluggishly. When a shower moves, the space it occupies becomes more oblong in the direction of motion and may be about 10 miles across. Thus showers – even over the sea – tend to form in boxes and make no man's lands between themselves and the next shower.

In this way millions of individual shower clouds develop, go through their life cycles and die over the water wastes of the Atlantic in mP airmasses. By the process of evolving latent heat (when the rising water vapour condenses into cloud) the warmth of the sea surface finds its way some thousands of feet aloft and forms another kind of inversion over a mP airmass that has spent a lengthy time at sea.

We can recognize such airstreams when small cottonwool cumulus clouds grow by day in bland westerly winds. *When the wind is in the west then the weather is at its best* says a well known weather jingle and it never gets better than on fair days with humble cumulus clouds that do not grow any larger because of the 'latent heat' inversion that the previous Atlantic history of the 'returning maritime Polar' (rmP) airmass has produced above them (compare photographs 5 and 8).

To sum up. The *Heat seeks cold* principle has led us to several different ways in which inversion layers can be created:

i inversions produced overnight by the cooling of the land
ii inversions produced by frontal activity so that warm air lies over cooler air
iii inversions due to release of latent heat when clouds form in great profusion

All inversions lead to stable layers, layer clouds or small heap clouds and a trend towards sinking air. The most prevalent cloud type to be found in inversions near the ground is stratocumulus. Inversions divide the wind above them from the wind below so that however strong the wind above an inversion layer, that below can be quite light and this is the situation to be found over the land from before sunset to after sunrise on many nights of the year. However inversion layers due to processes like iii above exist over the sea and produce the same resultant light wind regimes.

53 The way of the seabreeze

Sailing the coasts in spring and summer means the winds become complicated by the seabreeze forces that exist at these times of the year. On most fair days it is to be expected that the winds over the coastwise region will be shifted, calmed or reversed (or all three) during the morning or early afternoon. The further south you go the stronger will the seabreeze become so that whereas in British home waters (and related climes) you can expect a developed seabreeze to blow at some 10 to 12 knots in Southern and Mediterranean France it may habitually blow at 15 to 20 knots, while on the North African coast its more normal speed is some 25 knots.

Without at the moment going into why seabreezes blow, their major effects can be understood if we set down some simple facts. The best seabreeze days need plenty of sunshine, but they need not be hot. What is required for strong seabreeze forces to act is the formation of cumulus clouds. It is most important that the wind is not blowing too strongly against the seabreeze direction or the seabreeze system will not be able to stop and reverse it. The wind speed that will prevent the formation of the seabreeze is about the same as the speed of the breeze itself, ie about 10 to 12 knots. If you are cruising coastwise in the early forenoon and you would like to assess the chances of a seabreeze developing note the following factors:

figure 53.1

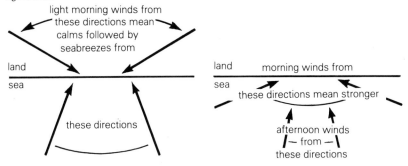

How the direction of the wind before the seabreeze modifies the wind in the afternoon, (a) when the morning wind is off-shore and (b) when the morning wind is on-shore.

   i is the wind blowing from a landward point? If it is, ask yourself
  ii how strongly is it blowing? If the speed is less than 10 knots ask
 iii is it sunny over the land or is the existing cloud likely to break up
     (upper clouds often break on summer mornings)? After that
 iv can you detect any cumulus clouds forming inland over hills or are
     there cumulus clouds about already?

Point iv is not absolutely essential to the establishment of seabreezes, but when you figure wind conditions are on the verge of making a breeze impossible the sign of cumulus developing makes it more likely that it could just happen. Regarding point iii, you can take it that seabreezes are possible on any day when sun, even broken sun, shines on an adjacent coast. It is the wind speed in the morning that is the controlling factor together with its direction, whether on-shore or off-shore (see page 31 for definitions of onshore, on-shore, offshore and off-shore).

The way the seabreeze affects the coastwise and landwise regions is quite different and depends on the wind direction with respect to the coast. The major facts are summarized in figure 53.1, but an on-shore morning wind can only be shifted to a point more perpendicular to the coast and be increased in speed by the seabreeze force 'pulling' on it from inland. There is very little more of value that can be said except to remember to allow for half a gusty gale in the afternoons of good seabreeze days that already have on-shore winds to help them.

The case when the wind has components from landward is quite different, if more complicated, but if coastwise cruising sailors are to obtain any value from knowing the way the seabreeze acts they are going to have to face the complexities. A wind blowing from the shore has first to be reduced to calm and then reversed by the local weather machine that

figure 53.2

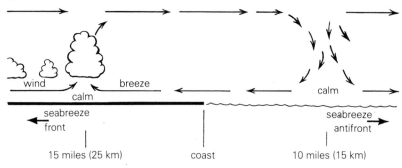

A seabreeze system in the middle of the afternoon.

powers the seabreeze. The process is of particular interest to coastwise cruisers as it happens within the first couple of miles of the shoreline which is their chief stamping ground. So let us describe the normal course of events around 0900 on a good seabreeze morning with a wind of about 6 to 8 knots (a light to gentle breeze) from the land (see figure 53.2).

You are a mile or so off a more-or-less straight coastline with a coastal plain. The visibility is quite good and while it is mainly sunny there are some cumulus clouds about. You assess this as a 'good seabreeze morning' and so are not surprised when the wind begins to desert you. It does not go all at once, but develops holes and odd calms interspersed with some stronger zephyrs. It is typically 1100–1200 by the time the coastwise waters are fully covered by this pregnant calm. We are waiting for the seabreeze.

It may become quite breathlessly calm with an 'oily' waveless swell, but then suddenly, even before you feel any breeze at all, you may be aware of shell-shaped catspaws covering the face of the sea. These are due to descending air currents from above and these falling currents help to erode any low cloud that may be in your vicinity so it becomes brilliantly sunny.

Then the breeze starts to come – a few wafts from seaward at first – followed by a more purposeful gathering of a light cool breeze that quickly strengthens to become gentle and eventually moderate in strength. Unless some strong disturbing influence, such as the gradient wind (see page 150) increasing markedly in strength, or the invasion of the coastal belt by showers or thunderstorms, comes along during the day, you can expect the whole of the coastal waters to be swept by a steady moderate breeze for the rest of the day. Its direction is often regular and well-known for the coast and a rule of thumb is that it will be from a point a little clockwise of straight on-shore. However there are exceptions to this rule so do not expect it to work every time.

While the waters inshore will be covered in a carpet of seabreeze the same cannot be said of further out because the calm area moves further offshore as the day progresses and sometimes is to be found as a region of flat calm lying as much as 20 miles out as the night comes on.

Further effects coastwise

The way a coastline faces will alter the way seabreezes act. A coast that faces southeast is going to see more sun on its slopes than one that faces west, for example. A coast with a coastal plain backed by hills is the best kind of terrain for absorbing early sunshine and so starting off the processes that result in seabreezes. Seabreezes will occur when there are cliffs or a steep-to shoreline rises out of the sea indented with coombes and estuaries, but they will not be as strong or organized as where there are good coastal plains and the higher ground starts further inland.

Thus the east coast and south coast of England have strong and regular seabreezes which push back winds from the NW quadrant behind strong seabreeze fronts (see figure 53.2). These are like miniature cold fronts and may set off showers or even thunderstorms as the breeze, forcing its way inland, meets the off-shore wind. Two air currents meeting more-or-less head on can only go upwards and the result is a line of deeper, darker cloud stretched along the seabreeze frontal line due to the ascending currents. However the seabreeze front is a landwise phenomenon and will not affect the coastwise or offshore fraternity.

West facing coasts will see less seabreeze activity than south- and east-facing ones because the sun does not shine on the inland slopes very early and the full potential for breeze formation is not reached until later in the day. By this time it is naturally waning anyway and another factor is that, with prevailing westerly winds, many of the seabreeze days are just those where the breeze adds to the wind already on-shore. However consider Liverpool Bay. Here the seabreeze system is very much in evidence as is its nocturnal counterpart the landbreeze and the seabreeze penetrates a long way up the Mersey and into the Cheshire Plain. Southport on this coast illustrates the way winds shift from day to night (see figure 53.3).

North-facing coasts see a curious phenomenon in that westerlies increase in strength and frequency on seabreeze days before they ever think of blowing inland. Equally easterlies along such coasts in the morning decrease in strength and frequency. There are seabreezes on these coasts just as there are on the north-facing shores of North Holland and Germany, and on the coasts of Normandy and Brittany that also face predominantly north, but they are not half as prevalent as on the seabreeze coasts of England. On the other hand the increase in westerly winds on sailing-season days at Cherbourg, for example, is very impressive. Statistics show that on early summer mornings some 27 hours out of every 100 are westerlies, but that by early evening this figure has increased to over 40 hours in every 100. That means seabreeze effects are at work during the

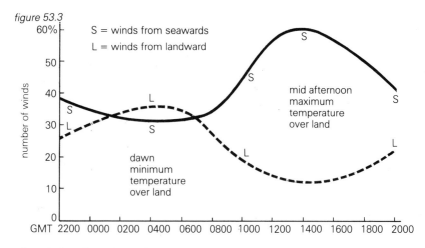

The wind regime of a typical coastal place.

day, not to haul the wind ashore, but rather to increase the frequency and speed of any winds that blow from the west parallel to the coast.

A remarkable example of this westerly effect is provided by wind statistics for Kiel whose waterway looks out NNE. It lies on the Baltic side of the Danish peninsula and so seabreezes ought to blow from the east or northeast and they do, but they do not in any way match up to the increase in westerly winds on summer days. To understand this remove Denmark from the map and then the whole sweep of coast from Terschelling to Gdansk is a north-facing seabreeze coast along which westerlies grow in response to seabreeze forces. What this means is that a narrow neck like the Danish peninsula is no barrier to the effect.

So when cruising coastwise you will be subject to many wind-shifts due to seabreeze forces and the results may not be as obvious as you might think. For example the seabreeze front that must develop between an off-shore wind and an on-shore seabreeze was said to be a phenomenon of the land that marches inland through the day pushing back the wind and allowing the breeze to penetrate many tens of miles inland on the best seabreeze days. However from the circulation of a developed breeze system as shown in figure 53.2 it is evident that there is another zone of calm or fitful winds some way out to sea due to the air sinking and flowing out to feed both seabreeze current and, further offshore, the off-shore wind that will still exist there. In effect the gradient wind can be considered to go over the seabreeze circulation and to come down again on the seaward side of it.

We can call the zone where the main sinking currents are to be found the 'seabreeze antifront' although it is not at all like its vigorous counterpart over the land. Because the air is sinking this antifront region may be a very

174

frustrating one for those who become caught in it and it may well be worth running the engine to get clear of it. However, just like the front inland, the antifront moves. It rolls out seaward with the day and to quote an example it can be found on summer evenings sprawling across the south of the Isle of Wight as a zone of total calm. Here it has moved some 15 miles from the main coastline and sometimes it may well get further seaward. So if the immediate coastal stretch next to the beaches is the place to avoid during the growth of the breeze in the morning then, when the breeze is established, that honour then belongs to the antifront zone further offshore while the inshore zone transforms into the best place to be to make passage with a soldier's wind. On good seabreeze days you have to go well offshore – perhaps 30 miles – to be sure of avoiding the calms and idle zephyrs of the seabreeze antifront. Even then you cannot be absolutely sure of avoiding the calms.

Seabreeze effects when the wind grows stronger

The descriptions and explanations given earlier of how seabreezes set in only dealt with days when the existing wind was already light or at the most moderate. The impression was given that when the wind in the early forenoon was more than about 10 knots no seabreeze effects could occur. This is manifestly not true, but what happens is that the existing wind is only shifted to blow more onshore than before. The wind statistics for any coastal place show this trend. For example the coast of the Low Countries between the Franco-Belgian border and the Frisians is a very windy one and Den Helder, opposite Texel, is the windiest place on the coast for which reliable statistics are available. From all seaward directions in the afternoons of the whole season there is often one chance in five that the wind will be Force 6 or above, but the on-shore seabreeze effect shifts winds that develop this strength out of the off-shore quadrants into the on-shore ones.

Or move down to Plymouth to find the statistics showing that while the seaward directions of between S and W gather to themselves some 36 per cent of the winds of all strengths at 0700, by 1300 in summer (and the same trend appears in spring and to a lesser extent in autumn) some 70 per cent of the winds are from these directions. This is a massive shift in winds that are not only light to moderate, but also fresh to strong as well.

The winds offshore will not be affected greatly by the seabreeze forces but the latter will act on them more and more as they blow across the coastline. The general effect on winds from NE and SE on an east-facing coast are shown in figure 53.4. Sailing coastwise will mean sailing fully close-hauled into the wind, but the further inshore you go on a sunny spring or summer day the freer you will become. Sailing with the wind on the quarter offshore will mean a more beam wind inshore.

Obviously this diagram a can be rotated to make it a south-facing or a

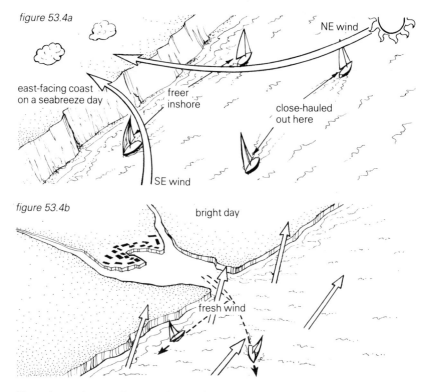

figure 53.4a

NE wind

east-facing coast
on a seabreeze day

freer
inshore

close-hauled
out here

SE wind

figure 53.4b

bright day

fresh wind

*How the seabreeze force acting on fresh winds (a) frees boats inshore
and (b) allows a new beating course when leaving harbour in the
middle of the day.*

west-facing coast and b illustrates leaving a south coast port in the middle
of the day with a wind that is fresh and from SW. Allowing for the change
of direction due to seabreeze forces you expect the wind to be from a more
westerly point further offshore so it may well be best to hold out on a long
starboard tack which will become more and more biased towards the
west as you get into deeper water. Again this diagram can be rotated to
represent an east coast with a SSE wind offshore or a west coast with a
NNW wind.

This is also an effect that helps in those long and frustrating flogs
up a coastline when the wind is dead against you and that is blowing
parallel to the coast. As the day progresses you will often find that on the
inshore legs you become freer and freer as you advance towards the
breakwaters and the bathers so that you will be able to make a long leg
along the shore before being forced to tack (see figure 53.5). Take as much
advantage of it as you can because as soon as the afternoon wanes, like a
leaf spring bent out of its normal position, the gradient wind will spring

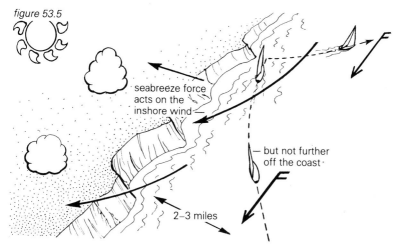

How the seabreeze force modifies winds blowing parallel to the coastline and allows long beating legs inshore but not offshore.

back to again flow parallel to the coast and probably drop somewhat in speed at the same time.

The above effect and others can be included in a universal rule when winds blow along coasts facing any direction. Assuming you are sailing off the coast *Face the coastline – a wind from the right hand will intensify by day and decrease by night. Cloud will tend to form over the coastal region.*

A wind from the left hand however will tend to decrease with the day and increase at night. Any cumulus type cloud will tend to disappear.

These winds have to be due to the gradient of the isobars and no other effect. Pursuing the topic further, when winds blow more directly on-shore or off-shore the following rules apply: *On-shore winds increase with the day and tend to build clouds over the coastal landmass. They decrease by night; Off-shore winds decrease with the day and cloud tends to disappear over the coastwise waters. These winds increase with the night.* (In this case we are talking of winds that are too strong to be stopped and reversed by the seabreeze forces – in effect that means winds of about 15 knots or above.)

54 The nocturnal wind

Winds for coastwise passage-making at night will nearly always tend towards becoming lighter. In particular when conditions are generally for 'winds, light and variable' the nocturnal wind may be all the coastwise wind there is. It consists of two effects that add together:

a the land breeze effect which is the night time analogue of the seabreeze by day
b katabatic winds that sink off coastal hills

The katabatics are due to cool night air sinking off the slopes that face the sea and making their way by any route they can find to the sea. They are very land-hugging and will tend to seek the minor creeks and writhes that penetrate into the landmass. They increase in speed with:

i height and steepness of the hill slopes
ii the proximity of the heights to the sea
iii the degree of cold to be found on the slopes

Thus where mountains look out across a coastal plain to the cruising venue always consider the risk of relatively strong night winds, especially when the gradient wind direction is already from the mountains. This effect reaches its maximum in the Mistral and Bora coastal slope winds of the Mediterranean, but lesser versions occur on Welsh and Scottish coasts for example.

The same clear 'radiation' nights that lead to katabatics also induce landbreezes so that it is often impossible to tell which is which and so we refer to them jointly as the 'nocturnal wind'. The return flow by night from land to sea is by no means as strong or uniform as the daytime seabreeze and if the nocturnal wind reaches 5 knots off coasts like the south coast of England you will be lucky. However on calm summer nights it may be all the wind there is. Stay inshore to get its main effects, slight as they are, and expect the 5 knots to be found in the first mile or two off the coastline to become progressively weaker as you go further out. At five miles off you will normally be beyond its sphere of influence.

Because it gathers itself by slipping down all the creeks etc that give it access to the sea, in an estuary you may well find the wind growing to as much as 10 knots by funnelling, but once clear of the headlands you may well lose it altogether. Locally it may become enhanced by falling down a coombe or other coastwise valley from higher ground inland and hills that are 20 or more miles away can still feed it.

The nocturnal wind usually starts after dark and takes a couple of hours to become initiated. It usually reaches its peak in the hours after midnight, but before dawn has lightened the horizon it will often be dead, leaving you to wallow through the first daylight hours until the sun begins to stir up the local land masses and so induce some air motion. Even then, on some occasions, you may not get any wind coastwise until the seabreeze begins to blow which it will do early in calm and sunny conditions.

55 Wind trends offshore

In the Baltic guarding the approaches to the Gulf of Bothnia lies a Finnish island called Ahvenanmaa and on its southwest corner is Maarianhamina. In summer (and to a lesser extent in other seasons) the south winds increase in frequency from about 15 per cent at 0800 to well over 50 per cent by 1400 and even at 2000 there is more than a 40 per cent chance of having a southerly wind. Maarianhamina is 30 miles from the coast of Sweden and 50 miles from that of Finland. It is therefore not exactly within the coastwise belt of either coast, yet there is this vast increase in winds from the south with the day.

It is an extreme example of a trend that will be found many, many miles from any coastline, but which is due to the sun's effect on adjacent land. In the Gulf of Bothnia it is caused by the many seabreeze currents that blow ashore round the shores of the Gulf which have to be fed from the Baltic which forms a great L-shaped 'valley' along which such winds will blow. Yet if you rob one piece of water of its surface air that piece will draw air from somewhere else to compensate.

So it is that we find Hammerhus on the island of Bornholm off the south coast of Sweden with a predominant trend towards W or SW winds in spring and summer. It is just responding to the 'vacuum' formed when winds blow up the Central Baltic to feed the Bothnian seabreezes – and breezes on to other Baltic coasts as well. No less than 75 per cent of winds at Bornholm are from W or SW on summer evenings. That means you have 3 chances out of 4 of having a wind from somewhere between SSW and WNW in this area at this time. And the trend feeds back and back through the Ostsee south of the Danish archipelago across the waist of the Danish peninsula and so into the North Sea. There we find a quite remarkable statistic for a sea area. Taken over the 24 hours there is a 50 per cent chance of having wind from the west in summer. Such a fact points to a form of 'monsoon' rather than a purely daytime trend and it is just one of several such 'monsoons' that feed across the watery wastes many miles from any landmass.

In my book *The Wind Pilot* (Nautical Publishing Company 1975), I described this tendency for the winds to blow out of the North Sea through the Ostsee and across Southern Sweden into the Gulfs of Bothnia and Finland as 'the westerly corridor' of winds. It is just part of the general monsoonal character of the winds in late spring and summer that tend to hug whatever waterways they can find as they feed out of the Atlantic into the European landmass. Winds will always blow along waterways if they can because even a rough sea is smoother than the land.

In figure 55.1 this westerly corridor is illustrated together with the most prevalent wind direction and its percentage frequency at midday in

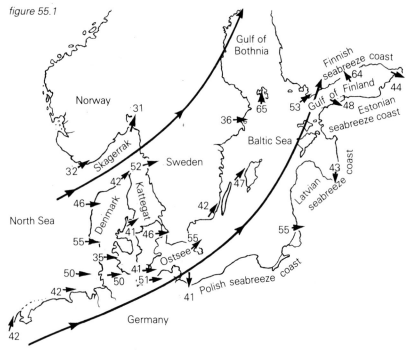

figure 55.1

Gulf of
Bothnia

Finnish
seabreeze coast
64
44
53 Gulf of Finland
48 Estonian
seabreeze coast

Norway
31

65

36

Baltic Sea

Skagerrak
32
52
Sweden
43
Latvian
seabreeze coast

42
47

Kattegat
46
Denmark
42

55
41
46
55

35
Ostsee
55

50
41
50
51

42
41
Polish seabreeze coast

Germany
42

North Sea

*The 'westerly corridor' of winds that sweeps through the Baltic Sea in
summer. The figures are percentage frequency from the most prevalent
wind directions in the middle of the day. At the entrance to the Gulf of
Bothnia (Maarianhamina) the 65% contains 50% from south. Note the
much lower frequency at the inland stations.*

summer. The Skagerrak in roughly the same direction helps to produce
the very high percentage (40 per cent) of SW winds on the coast between
Göteborg and Oslo Fiord. The diagram also shows the important effect of
shelter from such a strong trend in the winds. Along the Polish and
Latvian seabreeze coasts, wherever there is a promontory shielding a bay
from the west, the most likely wind is a seabreeze at midday whereas
without such shelter the most likely wind is from W or SW.

The Scilly Isles are some 25 miles from Land's End and of such small
extent that any seabreezes that blow on to them must be very limited. So
the winds we find there are really those of the Southwest Approaches.
Therefore you might not expect any very definite tendency for the wind to
increase from any particular direction with the day. Yet such is not the
case. There is a definite pick-up of winds from the west between morning
and afternoon/evening at St Mary's and this is evidence of the 'monsoon'
that feeds up the English Channel in summer and to a lesser extent in
spring, but which is absent in autumn, not surprisingly as winds at sea in

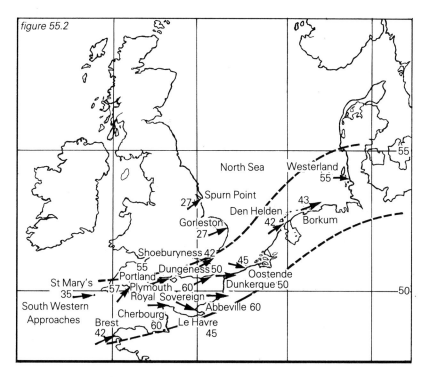

figure 55.2

North Sea

Westerland 55

Spurn Point 27

Den Helden 42

Borkum 43

Gorleston 27

Shoeburyness 42

Oostende 45

St Mary's 35

South Western Approaches

Portland 55

Dungeness 50

Dunkerque 50

Plymouth 57 60

Royal Sovereign

Abbeville 60

Cherbourg 60

Brest 42

Le Havre 45

The 'westerly corridor' starts in the South Western Approaches to the English Channel and then sweeps on into the Baltic. The numbers (as in fig 55.1) are percentage frequency of winds of all strengths surrounding the direction indicated eg the 57% figure at Plymouth is for winds between S and SW in the middle of the day in summer. At Oostende the direction is between W and NW etc. The trend is to have a very high percentage of winds from westerly points with a tendency to fan out on to adjacent land masses.

autumn show no direction to be much more likely than any other (see figure 55.2).

In gaining sea area Plymouth from Lundy it has been proved on several Fastnet races, that have been bedevilled by very light conditions, that there is more wind to be found by standing off and so increasing the chances of picking up the westerly monsoonal drift into and up the Channel. The existence of this other 'westerly corridor' up the Channel is shown by the statistics of wind at Royal Sovereign off Eastbourne. For while at dawn some 37 per cent of all winds are from SW or W this figure has increased to 60 per cent by the afternoon. Royal Sovereign is about nine miles off the coast, but is highly influenced by it for while SW is the most likely wind direction at dawn it is closely followed by the diamet-

181

rically opposite direction of NE at that time. This, of course, is the off-shore nocturnal wind asserting itself, but it is salutary to realize how far offshore it extends. It is only a night trend as is shown by the very few NE winds blowing in the afternoon. Those winds that were off-shore in the early morning have shifted to other directions of which SW is by far the most likely.

What happens at a position like that of Royal Sovereign off a coast with low hills – the South Downs come to an end at Beachy Head – is very typical of many other coastwise sea areas much frequented by cruising sailors. And the point is further strengthened when we find that west is the only direction that in any way approaches a frequency of one hour in a 100 for gales in summer. This frequency of about 1 per cent is reached in spring when SW joins W as a gale direction. Only in autumn do the gales begin to become frequent and by that time the only relatively gale-free directions are N and SE. In all there are some three hours of Force 8 or more winds in every 100 in the Channel in autumn, but that means that as the average duration of gales is some four hours, there are only about two gales in the average autumn month (see figure 10.1, page 46).

This example illustrates the way to look at statistics of gales. Only statistics for offshore areas are at all representative of the gale situation at sea and then the way the averages are arrived at means that winds over the whole 24 hours are included and so there is no way of knowing if there are specific daytime or night time trends. The latter can only be recognized from oceanic islands like Scilly, or Tiree which is some 25 miles off the broken coastline of Southwest Scotland. Another island that might be thought of as being offshore waters is Belle Ile, but this island is swept by the seabreezes of the South Brittany coast. A further point is that gale statistics for a sea area are gathered from as many different positions in it as possible, but most of the reports must come from ships or lighthouses whose routes or positions are very much fixed and are often not the zones frequented by yachts. Yachts will obviously avoid the shipping lanes and tend to hug the coastlines so that winds with on-shore or along-the-shore directions can create greater gale potentials than at sea, while winds from off-shore will often not reach gale proportions until they have fully shaken clear of the hamper of the land – and that may be many miles seaward. At the same time the big eddies induced by headland, promontory, and coastal cliff plus local enhancement of wind speed due to it blowing down coastal coombes and valleys may buffet the coastwise sailor, but will have lost much of this nasty variability by the time they get offshore. The time-honoured advice to go to sea to ride out the gale is seen here to be good.

Sometimes the trends mentioned in the tables between pages 184 and 186 will help to explain a wind direction that bears no relation to the one forecast for the sea area in question – and sometimes they won't. Occasionally odd, even quite considerable, winds spring up which it is difficult to pin on any obvious cause. However one prospect that should be considered is whether the winds may not be feeding an area of thunderstorms either locally or possibly far away. You can often assess whether this hunch is likely or unlikely from the feel of the weather or from a forecast for land areas.

56 Coastal winds through the 24 hours

When the big winds that build between lows and highs come along then local wind trends tend to be swept away before them, but with lesser winds and in particular with clear or partly cloudy conditions there will be definite tendencies for the coastwise winds to come from certain directions relative to the main coastline. In general the coastal wind principle is *Winds blow on-shore by day and off-shore by night* but this is an over-simplification. The night wind has a period when it is far more likely to blow than any other and there is a period before and surrounding dawn when the wind, whatever it is, tends to blow steadily without change of direction. As the sun rises the 'dawn wind' has to shift into the speed and direction it will have for the early forenoon and then there will often be another major change as the seabreeze effects act on the wind (see The way of the seabreeze, pages 170–2). Then the wind of the day will set in. By teatime the seabreeze effect is waning on south- or east-facing coasts and there may be a return to the morning wind direction or some entirely new direction. As the evening wears on there will often be a drop in wind speed or even calm and this occurs before the night wind begins to assert itself sometime after sunset. Then comes the highest prospect of nocturnal wind blowing from the land and we are back to where we started.

To help recognize the likely trends enter the following tables with your location eg off an east-facing coast and the time of day and read the trends. If the wind does not conform to them then you have too strong a gradient wind for them to modify it, or there is some local influence at work that cannot be allowed for in these simplified tables. Despite these provisos they will often help to explain an odd wind direction you have that does not seem to fit the pressure pattern.

Sailing off an east-facing coast

Period surrounding	Remarks
0200 GMT	Greatest chance of winds blowing from shorewards ie of nocturnal wind. If wind blowing on-shore this will probably be its time of lowest speed.
0400	This is the period of very little wind shift. The wind you have will probably last through dawn.
0600	Highest chance of wind blowing along the coast from a northerly point, or, if wind is southerly and persists that way, the time of lowest wind speed.
0900	Seabreezes may start if the period since dawn has been almost calm.
1200	Seabreezes will have started against winds that are light from the land. Stronger winds from landward decrease in strength in sunny or bright conditions. There may be local calms.
1500	Time of maximum wind from seaward or, if wind continues to blow from shorewards, the time of lowest off-shore windspeed.
1800	Greatest chance of winds blowing from a southerly point along the coast or, if the wind is northerly and persists that way, the time of lowest wind speed.
2200	Return to morning wind and the period of transition from seabreeze to nocturnal wind. Local calm.
2400	Nocturnal winds start to blow before midnight in many localities.

Sailing off a south-facing coast

Period surrounding	Remarks
0200	Period of maximum nocturnal wind.
0500	Period of very little wind shift.
0900	Highest chance of wind blowing from the east along the coast or, if the wind is persistently west, the time of lowest wind speed. This is also the period when the last of the night wind has to shift into the first of the morning wind.
1200	Seabreeze effects will be evident by this time if seabreeze has not already started to blow. Winds therefore tend to shift shorewards or there may be local calms.

1400	Highest chance of southerly winds or, if the wind persistently blows from a northerly point, the time of lowest wind speed.
1600	In sunny weather on-shore winds increase to maximum. Latest time for retarded seabreezes to start to blow. These cannot last long.
1800	Greatest chance of winds blowing along coast from the west or, if easterlies persist, the period of lowest wind speed.
2100	Period of transition from the last of the on-shore daytime wind to the off-shore nocturnal wind.
2400	Highest chance of wind from landward or on-shore winds tend to become less strong.

Sailing off a west-facing coast

Period surrounding	*Remarks*
0400	Period of very little wind shift.
0600	Commencement of the establishment of the morning wind on steep coasts; off-shore winds persist through this period.
0900	Greatest chance of winds from shorewards or time of lowest on-shore wind speed. With light airs on-shore seabreezes may start this early, but in general they will be delayed until later than on south- or east-facing coasts.
1200	Highest chance of winds from SW or time of lowest speed of NE winds. Seabreezes often set in before this time but when conditions are marginal for their incidence they are inclined to be later than on south- or east-facing coasts or may not occur at all.
1400	Period with greatest chance of seabreezes or, with easterlies, the time of lowest wind speed.
1600	Period of maximum on-shore wind speed. Winds already from seaward may become strong and gusty by this time. Seabreezes reach their maximum of frequency and speed.
1800	Afternoon wind wanes in strength, but in full glare of evening sun seabreezes continue to blow later on these coasts than on south- or east-facing coasts.
2000	Highest chance of winds from N or time of lowest speed of S winds.
2400	Period of growth of nocturnal wind against light on-shore winds or of strengthening off-shore winds of any strength.

Sailing off a north-facing coast

Period surrounding	Remarks
0300	Greatest chance of off-shore winds or of lowest on-shore wind speed.
0600	Period of very little wind shift.
0900	Seabreeze forces aid the increase in W winds and the decrease in E winds.
1200	Off-shore winds veer into W winds if moderate or more. If light they become seabreezes.
1400	Greatest chance of W winds and least number of E winds. Some seabreezes occur before this time, but conditions must be very conducive to their formation. Winds tend to veer (shift clockwise) with the afternoon.
1800	Seabreezes survive longer on this coast in high summer because the sun (now north of west) heats north-facing slopes. Or breezes may occur much later than would be expected on other coasts.
2000	Highest chance of on-shore winds. Fewest off-shore winds.
2200	Sudden shifts from seabreeze, often towards east. Greatest chance of easterlies. Lowest speed of W winds.

57 Wind effects along the coast

There are several important ways in which the wind speed and/or direction can be shifted by the features of the coastline; these are summed up in figures 57.1 and 57.2. Some of the effects have already been described, but here they are summarized for the two important cases when the wind is either mainly off-shore or on-shore.

Amongst the effects that can occur appear the following:

a The sheltering effect of the land. This should never be underestimated and when the wind is blowing from the land add up to two Beaufort forces to the wind speed you estimate in harbour by day and up to three by night. More specifically add a force to the land-retarded wind in the afternoon

The effect of land on the wind.

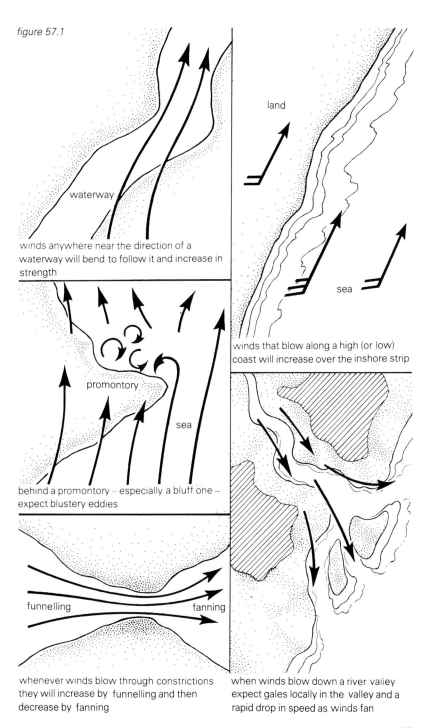

figure 57.1

winds anywhere near the direction of a waterway will bend to follow it and increase in strength

behind a promontory – especially a bluff one – expect blustery eddies

whenever winds blow through constrictions they will increase by funnelling and then decrease by fanning

winds that blow along a high (or low) coast will increase over the inshore strip

when winds blow down a river valley expect gales locally in the valley and a rapid drop in speed as winds fan

187

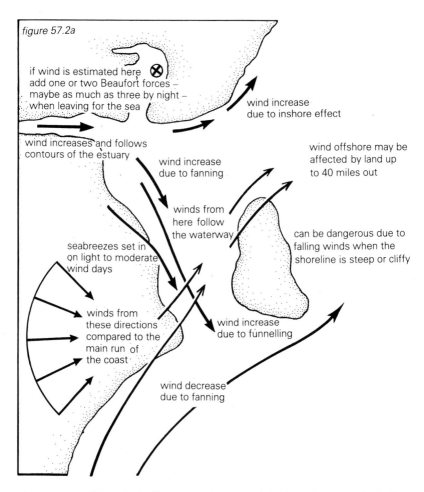

A summary of the wind effects near the coast (a) when the general wind direction is from the land and (b) when it is from the sea.

and two forces in the early forenoon and the evening. In overcast conditions at night add two Beaufort forces to estimate the wind at sea and, under clear skies with bright stars, add three forces. It is quite possible that Force 2 read under the influence of the land can be Force 5 when fully at sea. However that speed may not be fully realized until you are some tens of miles offshore.

b Fanning out of estuaries and bays. This will decrease the wind speed and change its direction as you stand out to sea. Conversely fanning will lead to increase in wind speed and a direction more closely guided by the confines of the shores as you beat in from seaward to enter a harbour or estuary.

188

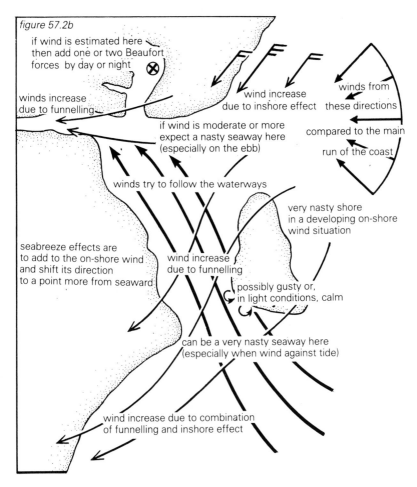

figure 57.2b

if wind is estimated here
then add one or two Beaufort
forces by day or night ⊗

winds increase
due to funnelling

wind increase
due to inshore effect

winds from
these directions

if wind is moderate or more
expect a nasty seaway here
(especially on the ebb)

compared to the main
run of the coast

winds try to follow the waterways

very nasty shore
in a developing on-shore
wind situation

seabreeze effects are
to add to the on-shore wind
and shift its direction
to a point more from seaward

wind increase
due to funnelling

possibly gusty or,
in light conditions, calm

can be a very nasty seaway here
(especially when wind against tide)

wind increase due to combination
of funnelling and inshore effect

c Funnelling. This will locally increase the wind speed as it tries to squeeze through a gap a few miles wide between say the mainland and an island.

d The inshore effect. This is the tendency of the wind to increase as it blows in a direction close to that of the shoreline. The wind will also be steered by the close proximity of the land.

e Falling winds. These are likely whenever the coastline is steep-to and the terrain rises rapidly out of the sea. It is seen at its most dangerous on lakes and lochs when thunderstorms or large showers suddenly appear over nearby ridges and cascade rain, hail and falling winds of gale force on to luckless sailors below. Normally no such prodigious onslaught occurs when sailing coastwise, but off hilly or mountainous coasts a weather eye should be kept for any obvious disturbance of air or water travelling from shorewards.

f 'Mistral' effects. The Mistral of the Gulf of Lions is a falling wind of vast proportions, but it illustrates the type of coastline and conditions that can cause larger than normal off-shore winds of a local nature. The factors that contribute to such winds as the Mistral are:

i high, cold mountain slopes inland

ii one or more constricting valleys to funnel air falling off the high slopes

iii a general isobaric gradient for winds in the general direction of mountains to coast

The Alps and the Rhône Valley contribute conditions i and ii so that the Mistral attains gale force over the northern coasts of the Gulf of Lions especially in spring. However its speed falls rapidly as it spreads further off-shore. It is at its most ferocious close inshore. In lesser places, hills with constricting valleys to the shoreline can provide local mini-Mistrals that, while not being of the scale or intensity of the Mediterranean wind, are certainly worth bearing in mind especially as they are most likely at night.

58 Thinking about the weather

The time of day when a forecast is made alters the points to be considered. Here is a 'think-tank' on what are the normal conditions and hints on what to think about at different times of day. L here means 'on land or with a land fetch', S means 'expect when there is a fetch from the open sea', / means 'later', x expect 'in next five hours', and C means 'consider'.

Dawn

Information   Tune in to early morning forecasts

Wind   L should be least x / increase and shift. S no change or some increase. x no change or some decrease. C changing pressure gradient-barometer?

Cloud   L least. There is no convection cloud at this time so any cloud is non-diurnal. In summer early cloud will often 'burn off'. x increase S most convection cloud. C encroaching or receding fronts

Precipitation   L at this time when continuous is frontal. Convective from seaward when showers. x die out but C the forecast. S as L when continuous but can be convective showers

Fog   L most likely time x burn off if clear above. Persist if cloudy above. S is sea fog and only wind or airmass change will disperse

Temperature   L lowest x increase and allow for wind chill. S low x change only with change of weather and in the sun
Humidity   L highest x sharp decrease S high and only airmass change really affects

0800–1000 LST (local sun time)

Information   Listen to breakfast time forecasts
Wind   L increasing but not markedly x increase with morning.
C seabreezes near coasts in light conditions
Cloud   L possibly low cloud developing. If clear x Cu to develop / showers? C forecast for fronts and pressure centre movements. S as Dawn but decreasing
Precipitation   L continuing or starting is frontal or high level convective. C if Cu growing already / showers? S as Dawn period
Fog   L radiation type should be going in summer – not always in winter. x clearance but if persists / afternoon clearance? C sea or frontal fog? S as Dawn period
Temperature   L increasing but if cool C showers x increase unless cloud and wind increase. Change of airmass? S as Dawn period
Humidity   L decreasing x and S as Dawn period C change of airmass

1200–1400 LST

Information   Listen to lunchtime forecasts
Wind   L increasing to maximum x strongest gusts C if applicable further increase due to tightening gradient or perhaps sudden decrease due to front passing etc. S expect major change only with change of pressure pattern
Cloud   L expect maximum low cloud x increase for a while / decrease C if unstable air can produce thunder or showers. There are airmass troughs at this time / clearing
Precipitation   L maximum showers but not thunderstorms. No variation in intensity of frontal precipitation middle of the day. Thundery showers tend to break out. x increase showers; thunderstorms / if conditions favour. C changes in frontal or cyclonic precipitation. S controlled by local fronts, sea temperatures and airmass stability. Showers may be at minimum
Fog   L expect minimum fog. Thus any fog is frontal, in advection fog or sea fog S fog is due to mT air over cool sea
Temperature   L maximum x decrease
Humidity   L minimum C if unusually high humidity, the reason S no diurnal variation at sea

1700–1900 LST

Information   Listen to teatime forecasts

Wind   L decreasing x calm evening in anticyclonic situation C increasing wind means cyclonic encroachment. S no marked diurnal change. C invisible gusts after dark – shorten canvas?

Cloud   L clearing skies, persistent cloud is frontal. Any storms tend to die out. x less low cloud overnight (although advection Sc can increase) S no diurnal variation

Precipitation   L showers die out. Storms may produce cloudbursts especially in hilly districts. Continuous precipitation is frontal. x dry night unless frontal precipitation

Fog   L increasing risk. Dusk is time of lowest visibility. x increase later C fog risk?

Temperature   L decreasing at maximum rate x slowing later S fall only by reason of loss of sun

Humidity   L increasing rapidly S no great change

2200–2400 LST

Information   Listen to late night forecasts

Wind   L minimum wind x land breezes near coasts C increasing S no diurnal change

Cloud   L no convection cloud but Sc can form in overnight inversion. High cloud is frontal but front need not be active C low St when mT air

Precipitation   L minimum showers. Precipitation is frontal – will it clear / ? (forecast?) x dry night unless frontal precipitation. C showers by dawn especially near coasts S maximum showers by dawn. See Lunchtime

Fog   L risk increases with the night x maximum around dawn. Decreasing wind and St becomes fog. C airmass change S sea or frontal fog but C St and poor visibility

Temperature   L decreasing to minimum around dawn. Frost risk increasing towards dawn C road icing in winter S fall only be reason of no sun

Humidity   L increasing to maximum by dawn. x dew especially in autumn

Appendix

How wind starts

Conditions at some altitude have to alter before a surface wind may start. Wind at sailing level is nearly always the result of a change in the upper air. Before surface air pressure can fall one or both of two different effects must occur:

  i the average density of the air above must decrease ie the column must, on the whole, get warmer

 ii more air must flow out of the air column above where the pressure is falling than flows into it. This is a situation called *divergence*

Conversely for pressure to rise:

 iii the average density must increase ie the column must, on the whole, become colder

 iv more air must flow into the air column above where the pressure is rising than flows out of it. This situation is called *convergence*

In most situations the origin of the wind that blows cannot be traced easily, but it can when a seabreeze starts. As seabreezes need light winds that will not oppose them too strongly so, as in figure A.1, it is perfectly reasonable to think of the pressure sprawled across the coastline as uniform. Let it be 1000 mb in the early morning and let there be little or no wind from any other cause.

As the sun rises the air over the land is warmed and has to expand. It can only do so upwards. The air over the sea remains the same as before. From the figure it is seen that, for example, the 900 mb pressure level is higher up in the warm column over the land than in the cold one over the sea. So there is a pressure gradient, albeit a weak one, from the land to the sea above the surface as the sun heats up the land. Thus air flows out of the column over the land (divergence) and the pressure at the surface can fall. The air flows into the column over the sea (convergence) and the pressure at the surface rises.

Thus, small, and actually undetectable, air motions from land to sea at altitude account for the surface pressure difference that initiates the seabreeze. As we cannot put a ceiling on how high the effect of expansion over the heating land can extend, very low wind speeds flowing out aloft can allow for the 10 or more knots experienced in a shallow surface seabreeze which is, very often, only a few hundred feet deep.

Conversely a landbreeze is due to the cooling and settling of the air over the land on clear, radiation nights. Now any pressure level near the surface is found at a lower level over the land than over the sea, where the pressure levels do not appreciably alter. There is now a tendency for the air aloft to ease in over the land so reducing pressure by divergence over the sea. The surface current – the landbreeze – is the result. Again it needs very quiet conditions to obtain before the landbreeze is appreciable and only rarely is it anywhere near as strong as the seabreeze.

Thus here winds can be seen being born and developing due to temperature differences in air columns. Similar effects on a much grander scale produce the large-scale winds of the world, but they do not blow straight from high to low pressure because of the effect of the Earth's rotation. Even in the case of the seabreeze there is a tendency to véer with the day so that on a south-facing coast the breeze, which started off blowing directly on-shore is, by late afternoon, coming from the southwest or even west. Thinking about it, you can see that the breeze is trying to end up blowing with low pressure on its left as all established winds do in the northern hemisphere. In the southern hemisphere the effect will be the reverse.

By contrast the fall in pressure that initiates a depression centre is usually a mixture of density change and divergence over a 'wave' in the Polar Front which is where most depressions start.

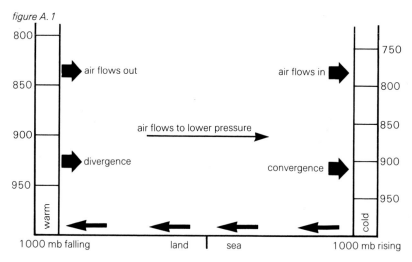

figure A. 1

Wind starts by air motion in the higher air decks and this induces wind at the surface.

UK broadcast forecasts

The major shipping forecasts are broadcast four times a day at 0015, 0625, 1355 and 1750 (clock times). They include a statement of gale warnings in force, a general synopsis covering the next 24 hours and likely changes, forecasts for the following sea areas giving wind direction and speed, weather and visibility: Viking, Forties, Cromarty, Forth, Tyne, Dogger, Fisher, German Bight, Humber, Thames, Dover, Wight, Portland, Plymouth, Biscay, Finisterre, (Trafalgar only at 0015), Sole, Lundy, Fastnet, Irish Sea, Shannon, Rockall, Malin, Hebrides, Bailey, Fair Isle, Faeroes, South-East Iceland.

Actuals for the following coastal stations are included if time allows: Tiree, Sumburgh, Bell Rock, Dowsing, Goeree, Varne, Royal Sovereign, Channel Lightvessel, Scilly, Valentia, Ronaldsway and Malin Head. Jersey is also included sometimes. Actual elements reported are wind direction and force, present and past hour weather, visibility and where available sealevel pressure and tendency.

Inshore waters forecasts for England and Wales are broadcast on Radio 4 after midnight and on Radio 3 in the early morning. They cover a period about 18 hours ahead and a coastal strip about 12 miles wide. The Radio 4 broadcast includes actuals from the following stations: Boulmer, Spurn Point, Manston, Channel Lightvessel, Lizard, Mumbles, Valley and Blackpool.

Inshore waters forecasts for Scotland are broadcast by BBC Radio Scotland at 2340 weekdays and 2330 weekends. They give a summary of gale warnings for all sea areas north of 55°N and include actuals for 2200 from Machrihanish (Kintyre), Tiree, Stornoway, Sule Skerry, Aberdeen, Leuchars and Lerwick.

Inshore waters forecasts for Northern Ireland are broadcast by BBC Radio Ulster and are similar to the above. They include the 2100 and 2200 actuals from Kilkeel, Malin Head, Machrihanish, Valley and Orlock Head.

The locations of these stations are shown on the map opposite.

BBC local radio stations in many cases give extensive local forecasts that are directed towards small craft and it is to these rather than the sparse and generalized shipping and inshore waters forecasts that the local mariner should look. These stations broadcast both on medium wave and VHF. They comprise Radios Birmingham, Blackburn, Brighton, Bristol, Carlisle, Cleveland, Derby, Humberside, Leeds, Leicester, London, Manchester, Medway, Merseyside, Newcastle, Nottingham, Oxford, Sheffield, Solent and Stoke-on-Trent.

BBC Television provides brief coverage of nationwide weather and its regional programmes do little to supplement the national picture. However the Atlantic chart is shown once or twice a day for a period of a few seconds enabling a general impression to be gained. The more detailed coverage designed to be colour-visual and for the mass audience uses the symbols given on page 99. It is possible that the ITV alternative coverage may be better for local weather although this is not true in a fair proportion of cases. Times of weathercasts should be looked up in *Radio Times* and *TV Times*. In this context see the sections on Teletext and Viewdata systems. BBC regional TV stations include East Anglia, Midlands, North, Northeast, Northwest, South, Southwest and West.

Coast Radio Stations

One of the most useful Coast Radio Stations in the southern North Sea is the Dutch station of Scheveningen just north of 's Gravenhage. At the time of writing (and this is not likely to change) the schedule is: Scheveningen (W/T callsign PCH) 1939 and 2824 kHz plus Channel 14 VHF (all R/T).

Gales are announced on receipt and at end of next silence for Netherlands coastal waters and North Sea generally. There are weather forecasts including the gale situation (Force 7 and above) at 0340, 0940, 1540 and 2140 GMT in English and Dutch for Netherlands coastal waters up to 30 miles offshore, the Ijsselmeer and the North Sea. There are also actual weather reports from local stations.

While it is not possible to give detailed schedules for all the Coast Radio Stations that broadcast in English it is worth noting that British stations broadcast at 0803 or 0833 and 2003 or 2033 GMT. The full schedules can be found in the *Admiralty List of Radio Signals* (Vol 3) and resumés are to be found in nautical almanacs and the RYA 'Weather Forecasts'. For locations and frequencies see figures 5.2 and 5.3 (pages 32–4).

Locations of weather centres in Britain and 'actuals' stations around Britain and the North Sea.

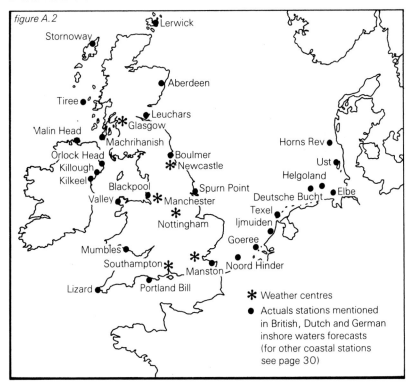

figure A.2

* Weather centres
● Actuals stations mentioned in British, Dutch and German inshore waters forecasts (for other coastal stations see page 30)

Names of sea areas in other languages

British	French	German	Danish/Spanish
Viking	Viking (Offshore)	Viking (North)	Vikingbanke
	Utsire (Inshore)	Nördliche Nordsee Ostteil (South)	
Forties		Nördliche Nordsee	Fladengrund (Offshore)
Cromarty	Fladen Ground	Westteil	Jaerens Rev
Forth			Sydvest (Inshore)
Tyne	Tyne	Mittlere Nordsee Westteil	
Dogger	Dogger Bank		Doggerbanke
Fisher	Fisher Bank	Mittlere Nordsee	Fiskerbankerne (Offshore)
		Ostteil	Vesterhavet (Inshore)
German Bight	German Bight	Deutsche Bucht	Tyskebugt (Offshore) Helgolandsbugten (Inshore)
Humber	Humber	Sudwestliche	Brunebanke
Thames	Sandette	Nordsee	
Dover	Manche Est	Englischer Kanal Ostteil	
Wight			
Portland	Manche Ouest	Englischer Kanal Westteil	
Plymouth			
Biscay	Ouest Bretagne (North)		Vizcaya (North and Centre)
	Nord Gascoigne (Centre)		
	Sud Gascoigne (South)		Cantábrico (South)
Finisterre	Cap Finisterre		Finisterre
Sole	Sole		
Shannon			
Fastnet	Sud Irlande		Gran Sol
Lundy			
Irish Sea	Mer d'Irlande	Irische See	
Rockall	Ouest Irlande		
Malin	Nord Irlande		
Bailey			
Hebrides	Ouest Ecosse		
Fair Isle		Shetland	Papabanke
Faeroes			Farvendet omkring Fairøerne

Important words to listen for in French and Spanish forecasts

English	French	Spanish
Gale warning	Avis coup de vent	Aviso de temporal
Gale	Coup de vent	Viento duro
Storm	Tempête	Temporal
Strong	Fort	Fuerte
Fresh	Fraîche	Fresco
Wind	Vent	Viento
Veering	Virement ou virage	Dextrogiro
Backing	Recul de vent	Rolada a la izquierda
Six	Six	Seis
Seven	Sept	Siete
Eight	Huit	Ocho
Nine	Neuf	Nueve
Ten	Dix	Diez
North	Nord	Septentrional, boreal
South	Sud	Sur
East	Est	Este
West	Ouest	Oeste
Increasing	Augmentant	Aumentar
Decreasing	Affaiblissant, diminuant	Disminución
Deepening depression	Cruesement dépression	Ahondimento depressión
Deep depression	Profond dépression	Profundo depressión
Fog	Brouillard	Niebla
Dense	Dense	Denso
Mist	Brume légère	Neblina
Visibility	Visibilité	Visiblilidad
Poor	Mauvais	Mal
Weather	Temps	Tiempo
Forecast	Prévision	Previsión
Weather report	Rapport, bulletin méteorologique	Boletin meteorologico
Thunderstorm	Orage	Trueno

Index